THE LOGIC OF DIPLOMACY

D1608056

RECENT VOLUMES IN
SAGE LIBRARY OF SOCIAL RESEARCH

THE LOGIC OF DIPLOMACY

ALAN S. ALEXANDROFF

FOREWORD BY
RICHARD N. ROSECRANCE

Volume 120
SAGE LIBRARY OF
SOCIAL RESEARCH

 SAGE PUBLICATIONS   Beverly Hills   London

For information address:

SAGE Publications, Inc.
275 South Beverly Drive
Beverly Hills, California 90212

SAGE Publications Ltd
28 Banner Street
London EC1Y 8QE, England

Printed in the United States of America

Library of Congress Cataloging in Publication Data

Alexandroff, Alan S.
    The logic of diplomacy

    (Sage library of social research ; v. 120)
    Bibliography; p.
    1. Diplomacy—Research.   2. International re-
lations—Research.   I. Title.
JX1662.A64   327.2'072   80-29544

ISBN 0-8039-1572-1
ISBN 0-8039-1573-X (pbk.)

FIRST PRINTING

CONTENTS

120751

To Blanche Axton Alexandroff

ACKNOWLEDGMENTS

The number of people who have been supportive of this project while it evolved from an idea to a dissertation to this volume is legion. Nevertheless, there are some whose help has been so substantial and so appreciated by me that I cannot miss the opportunity to acknowledge them here.

First, I must make mention of the many members of the Departments of Government and History at Cornell and the London School of Economics and Political Science who made me appreciate the intricacies of international politics. In particular, I'd like to thank Professors M. Anderson, James Joll, E. W. Kelley, Knight Biggerstaff, David Mozingo, E. W. Fox, P. J. Katzenstein and Richard N. Rosecrance. Of those gentlemen, particular thanks must go to members of my special committee—E. W. Fox, P. J. Katzenstein, E. W. Kelley, and most especially Richard N. Rosecrance. All four provided valuable criticism as the research and writing proceeded. But to Richard Rosecrance, committee chairman, I can never fully express my thanks for the intellectual stimulation as well as collegial support he provided through the various stages of this project and in my years at Cornell.

Since my return to Canada, various colleagues have provided valuable critiques of all or portions of the manuscript. These individuals include J.A.W. Gunn of Queen's and Harald von Riekhoff of Carleton. Special thanks is also due James de Wilde, whose presence and intellectual eagerness are responsible for creating an environment here at Queen's in which it was possible to carry on the intellectual and pedogogic tasks.

For emotional support through the various stages of this project I must pay homage to my mother and father, who always kept me encouraged; my dear friends from college—Christopher Harmer, Jean Sands and Gail Harris; and my Ithaca family—all the Rosecrances, particularly Barbara Rosecrance. Finally, and certainly not least, I must thank Blanche Axton Alexandroff.

For financial assistance I must thank the Canada Council, now the Social Science and Humanities Research Council. Their doctoral fellowship program provided me with four valuable years of graduate assistance. Thanks must also go to Nancy Sokol of Cornell, who was invaluable in getting the earlier manuscript typed and conveying messages between Queen's and Cornell. Jane Dreeben was of inestimable assistance.

To these people and many others I express my greatest appreciation. Needless to say, I remain totally responsible for any errors of fact or interpretation that may still exist in this book.

A.S.A.

FOREWORD

Richard N. Rosecrance

The study of quantitative international politics has largely reached an impasse. Few significant findings have resulted from contemporary research. Negative findings have been more characteristic of quantitative efforts than positive conclusions, and the positive findings of some scholars often have not been endorsed by others using different techniques over a variety of historical periods. Some investigators have therefore decided that quantitative efforts are not likely to lead to productive conclusions and have abandoned the quest. It is a signal strength of the work of Professor Alan Alexandroff that he has sought to push quantitative efforts further, to use them more discriminatingly, and to tie them more closely to historical research in an effort to reach new and more satisfying results. The study that follows is a reflection of such beliefs and efforts. Despite all the obstacles, it is surprisingly successful and breaks new ground in a number of respects.

Methodologically, it is one of the first studies to encompass the entire range of international outcomes, from cooperation to conflict. The hypotheses charted in the study are tested against a "normal curve" of international behavior, not merely against the extremes of that curve: "war" and "crisis" on the one hand, and/or "alliance" on the other. Second, because of the nature of the Situational Analysis Project data set, Alexandroff could easily compare general empirical conclusions with the specific diplomatic actions that were causing the results in question.

Systemic findings could be mirrored in particular national behavior. Third, since the data set covers the diplomacy of the
European great powers in the period 1870-1890, it was possible
to examine the policy of each major state in ways that both
reflected and, to a degree, transcended the findings of diplomatic historians.

In substantive terms, Alexandroff seeks to press beyond the
typical "attribute" explanations of international behavior, war,
and peace. According to the conventional mode of inquiry,
actions are the result of patterns of power, status, alliance,
alignment, or of other "fixed" characteristics of the actors or of
their relationships. This approach has been singularly unsuccess-
ful in other studies, and it should not have been expected to
explain the subtle diplomacy of the generation from 1870 to
1890. In contrast, he uses diplomatic behavior as an independent as well as a dependent variable; for it is possible that the
best and most consistent explanation for the behavior of one
particular actor, B, is the behavior of actor A toward him. In a
fully "symmetrical" behavioral system, each power would return precisely the amount of cooperation and conflict that it
received from others. This, after all, was the premise of arms-
race hypotheses and the basis of the "conflict spiral" model
which results from the interaction of "threat" and "counterthreat." The "symmetry hypothesis" is strikingly vindicated in
Alexandroff's study. Most of what states do is explained by
what other states do to them, though this is more strongly the
case in cooperative than in conflictual actions. The lower degree
of "symmetry" in the conflict spectrum, of course, tempts one
to believe that the "deterrence hypothesis" may best explain
the residual outcomes: nonsymmetry exists when strongly conflictual actions are met with cooperative responses. In fact, this
did not turn out to be the case. The more strongly conflictual
actions did not elicit cooperative responses: rather, a threat-
counterthreat pattern could be observed in such instances.

Despite the general adequacy of the "symmetry hypothesis,"
its failure to explain all cases and the failure of the "deterrence
hypothesis" to supplement it on the conflictual side leads

Alexandroff to inquire into additional structural explanations
of the events in question. It may be that the different patterns
of symmetry are to be accounted for in terms of different
power, status, alliance, or alignment of the parties in question.
The results of such a test, however, show that crude "attribute"
interpretations of symmetry do not explain the residual variance. Alliance dyads are not necessarily less symmetrical in
responses than nonallied powers. "Power" does not explain the
symmetry of behavior; nor it is true that "the higher the joint
status of dyad A and B, the higher the symmetry of cooperation
and the lower the symmetry of conflict." The "status inconsistency" hypothesis also bears no apparent relation to symmetry
of behavior. It is only when Alexandroff turns to de facto
relations of "alignment" in Chapter Six that the first really
significant positive findings emerge. There he finds a strong
relationship between symmetry and de facto cooperative (alignment) relations between powers. States which are highly cooperative have low conflictual symmetry and high cooperative
symmetry. Such cooperative alignment patterns, however, by
no means reflect formal alliance. Alexandroff points out that
the "uses of Alliance" are many and that they sometimes
involve ties among states which would otherwise move toward
mutual hostility. In practical terms, the linkage between Austria
and Russia in the Three Emperors' Alliance was designed by
Germany to overcome, or at least to dampen, hostile rivalries in
the Balkans. The Russo-German Reinsurance Treaty of 1887
(from which Austria was excluded) was designed to truncate a
developing Russian relationship with France. It was only par-
tially successful. Indeed, one of the most historically interesting
conclusions of the Alexandroff work is that the origins of the
Franco-Russian alliance were firmly implanted in the Bismarckian period. One can observe the developing entente between the
two "outcast" powers even during the last years of the German
Chancellor's ascendancy.

It is nonetheless true that Bismarck's "balance of diplomacy"
did manage to hold a refractory international system together
when a variety of tendencies, not least those of colonial rival-

ries, were conspiring to drive it apart. The German Chancellor aimed to counterbalance existing polarities or insistent friendships, fashioning a "mixed international system." Russia and Austria were supposed to get on with each other through the mediation of the friendly confidant of both: Germany. Russia and England were kept from coming to blows. Bismarck's only failure was to effect a rapprochement with France. He held out vistas of colonial expansion, conjoined with common action against Britain, but these held no last attractions to the French, who kept their sights focused on the Rhine. Nonetheless, the very "inconsistency" of Bismarck's alignments brought rivals together and constrained their aggressive impulses. The German diplomatist also did not give free rein to cooperative tendencies between particular powers. Austria needed Germany's help to rebuild her position, both domestically and also against Russia, but Berlin never allowed the friendship of the two Germanic powers to limit cooperation with others. Austria was forced to accept Russia as well as Italy. England and Austria were kept at arm's length in most instances, where they had common interests against Russia. France's old ties with Vienna were broken and the new ones with St. Petersburg were held in suspended animation. The mixed international system prevented polarization; "cross-cutting cleavages" managed to link powers in a web of diplomatic ties that inhibited forthright national aggression. Colonial expansion became the surrogate for gains in Europe; but, as Alexandroff correctly shows, these added to the strains on the diplomatic mechanism and produced long-term complications.

The application of these notions in the 1980s is quite different from what political leaders would often have us believe. As Alexandroff points out, it is easy to conclude that the playing of the "China card" will put pressure on the Soviet Union and bring a chastened Moscow to the negotiating table. Such prospects, however, have little contemporary or historical validity. Russia was not drawn into cooperative diplomacy by such means in the 1880s. Indeed, when Bismarck's successor, Caprivi, tried to play the "English card," it only drove Russia into the arms of France. It was because Bismarck did not take sides between St. Petersburg and Vienna that he managed to remain on good terms with each. Neither had to conclude that the scales of power had turned irrevocably against it. In contemporary terms, this suggests a more even-handed balancing of Russia and China than has yet been attempted, even by Kissinger. Bismarck was willing to use rearmament to press his foes toward cooperation, but he never relied on this means alone.

In the Middle East Alexandroff hazards the view that the policy of excluding Moscow and the radical Arabs may frustrate a comprehensive agreement. Yet the Iraq-Iran war has discredited Syria as well as Iran and probably given America added leverage to produce a settlement. Even the Egypt of Sadat may gain a renewed diplomatic potency. But this possibility does not vitate his general claim that in the Middle East, as elsewhere, the "balance of diplomacy" requires even-handedness. Key actors in a settlement cannot be expected to honor it if they are left out until the final stages. Only if the USSR and Syria (as well as the Palestine Liberation Organization) are truly irrelevant in Middle East politics and power can their interests and presence be ignored. In sum, even a Reagan Administration eventually will come to see that the route to strategic equilibrium and a Middle East agreement passes through Moscow as well as other capitals.

Alexandroff opts for a "multipolar" system of cross-cutting rivalries and friendships in preference to the oft-preferred "bipolarity." This is presumably because a "bipolar" system unmediated by countervailing linkages produces an action-reaction phenomenon and a spiraling arms race as well. "Balance of power" cannot be the necessary and sufficient condition of international stability and peace; the latter depends on a "balance of friendship" which sustains—and legitimizes—the power balance. Nations, despite argument to the contrary, do not work cooperatively with one another merely because of the dictates of power. There must also be sufficient respect and reciprocity to prevent them from falling into isolation, apathy, and resignations—conditions which frequently provoke war.

In sum, Alexandroff offers a stimulating new analysis which attempts to rehabilitate quantitative analysis in international relations by using a much more disciplined and discriminating fashion. No correlations are essayed, only paired comparisons. The results suggest that crude attributes do not predict the behavior of nation-states, but that actions are themselves the cause of reactions. The symmetry hypothesis is largely validated. De facto alignments turn out to be much more important than attribute variables in charting a "balance of diplomacy." Many questions remain to be answered, particularly about the specific effect of different diplomatic patterns on the outcomes of the international system. But the general tendency leans in the right direction: toward the more subtle and discrete analysis of international politics.

Chapter 1

INTRODUCTION

Contemporary quantitative analysis of international relations has neglected the historical role of diplomacy. Efforts to depict the patterns of diplomacy—are absent or only perfunctorily treated in such analyses. Instead, historical outcomes are explained in gross terms of measured power, status, or alliance aggregation—the easily quantified structural elements of international politics. Diplomacy has gone largely unexamined, because it is so much more difficult to quantify.

This study tried to accomplish two objectives. First, it endeavors to examine in a systematic and rigorous way the patterns of diplomatic behavior among the European powers of the period—1870 to 1890. It places diplomacy at the heart of the explanation and it asserts that there are patterns that historians and political scientists have ignored. In order to establish this claim, the examination begins with the influence of nation A's behavior on the behavior of nation B. We need to know whether diplomatic interaction is symmetric, whether a nation's threats lead to threats, whether cooperation leads to cooperation.

Many quantitative studies have subjected crudely defined historical data from a series of continents and time periods to general regression and factor analytic techniques. The second objective of this analysis is to offer a "discrete analysis" of diplomatic patterns in the European state system from 1870 to 1890. Unlike systemic analyses, which provide only broad and uninterpretable correlations, in the examination which follows, we can move quickly from the broad quantitative results to the actual and particular diplomatic events and actors which caused the results. Thus, each quantitative finding, each hypothesis verified or refuted, can be explained by quick reference to the actual happenings of the diplomatic period. As a result, this study can remain sensitive to both the diplomacy and the structural characteristics of the Great Powers. This discrete analysis permits a focus on diplomacy while extending the range of quantitative international relations.

As a result of these theoretic and methodological objectives, the study seeks to remain in touch with both historical and quantitative perspectives. It fully develops the descriptive historial approach in an analysis of the logic of diplomacy and captures the complex diplomacy of Germany/Prussia, France, Great Britain, Russia, Austria-Hungary, and Italy, the European Great Powers in these two crucial nineteenth-century decades. Then, we use the scales and techniques developed by the Situational Analysis Project to obtain a universe of events to test in a precise manner the logic of diplomacy—the patterns of symmetry of Great Power interaction. Our results show that symmetry is indeed a major characteristic of European diplomatic interaction. Since both conflict and cooperation are symmetric the study calls into question notions of behavioral deterrence. The analysis reveals that the behavior of one State may be a major determinant of the behavior of another State in the international system.

The dual historical and quantitative approach also allows us to carry further structural or attribute analyses of outcomes in international relations. Quantitative international relations has focused on structural characteristics to explain behavior in international politics. We examine the explanatory power of structural explanations in light of our findings on the symmetry of interaction. In the analysis, we employ the most frequently identified structural characteristics—power, status, and alliance. The 1870-1890 period of European diplomacy is frequently regarded as a model representative of classic concepts of the balance of power and alliance. It is a period when Realpolitik predominates under Disraeli, Gorchakov, Andrassy, and most especially, Otto von Bismarck. It is all the more revealing, therefore, that none of the structural variables are systematically capable of explaining the patterns of interaction. In fact, only a less formal structural variable—alignment—consistently and significantly relates to the patterns of Great Power symmetry. The discrete analysis allows us to show why the structural variables fail to explain the patterns of diplomacy. It also suggests more dynamic "structural-behavioral" variables. Thus, we no longer focus on the formal structural variable alliance but "alliance use"; we focus not on the balance of power but on the balance of diplomacy.

The findings in this particular period call into question the structural approach so favored by international relations specialists in other periods. The importance of symmetry and less formal structural variables underscores the need for greater attention to the logic of diplomacy and to the informal mechanisms of international politics in the contemporary setting. As we shall see later, the Superpowers may find a "mixed relationship" the best means of avoiding conflictual outcomes in diplomatically delicate situations. This study, I believe, provides policy makers as well as analysts with new insights into an explanation of outcomes in world politics. Though only a first step on a very difficult road to knowledge, it is hoped that this volume will serve as a catalyst for further gains in explaining the diplomatic workings of the international system.

Chapter 2

BEHAVIOR IN INTERNATIONAL RELATIONS THEORY

This analysis focuses on nation-state behavior and, more explicitly on the symmetry of interaction. A review of the international relations literature reveals, however, that there has been too little attention devoted to this concept. This study contends that the concepts of interaction and symmetry of behavior are at the core of explanations of outcomes in the international system. From the diplomatic record it is apparent that some threats lead to a reduction in conflict between states, while other threats lead to a vicious cycle of threat and counterthreat. Cooperative behavior may lead to increased demands and threats, or to increased cooperation.

The inability to predict an adversary's response is a major problem in international relations and a limitation in our understanding of nation interaction. If credible threats, for instance, could be shown invariably to lead to positive responses, this knowledge would improve immeasurably our understanding of the outcomes of international relations. Yet even a superficial

survey of international politics suggests bewildering and contra-
dictory patterns of interaction. President Kennedy, for instance,
gambled in Cuba in 1962 that American threats in response to
Soviet emplacement of missiles there would result, ultimately,
in a cooperative response by Chairman Khrushchev. Lord Grey,
in 1914, hoped that British threats to enter the war would end
positively in Germany's evacuation of Belgium. In the first
example, President Kennedy's calculations were proven correct;
in the second case, Lord Grey's threat failed to elicit a cooperative German response. While tensions eventually eased in the
Cuban missile crisis, in 1914, war was the ultimate result.

The uncertainty of our understanding of responses character-
izes all international situations, not just crisis. Our efforts to
uncover the logic of diplomacy force us to look at the ongoing
interaction, not just at the narrow range of crisis behavior. We
can see crisis outcomes as part of a larger pattern of diplomacy.
Thus, *ab initio,* we lack knowledge of whether Bismarck's
threats invariably return French threats or bring French compliance; we remain in the dark when it comes to understanding
whether Great Britain's cooperation leads to Austro-Hungarian
or Russian cooperation or demands. We remain at a loss to
understand the patterns of diplomacy of all these powers—
Prussia/Germany, Great Britain, France, Russia, Austria-Hungary, and Italy—in these twenty-one years.

Since diplomacy was a central feature in this period and in
the contemporary international system, it is hard to understand
why previous analysis has been so neglectful of it. To avoid
earlier shortcomings and to build on those significant efforts
already achieved in international relations theory, perhaps a
brief assessment of current research would be valuable. The
following section offers a critique of previous and ongoing
approaches, but it also represents an effort to illustrate the
requirements of a systematic yet discrete analysis of interstate
interaction. It tries to place behavior and interaction at the
center of explanation in quantitative international relations
while still building on other valuable research in the field.

APPROACHES TO INTERSTATE BEHAVIOR
AND INTERACTION

THE HISTORICAL APPROACH

Diplomatic history, at least till the end of World War II, remained the major approach to the study of behavior in international relations. Diplomatic historians, attempting to explain the outcomes of international politics, particularly peace and war, examined in great depth the events of interstate politics. With skill, they investigated the objectives of statesmen in times of tension, war, appeasement, and détente—indeed, all the situations and circumstances of world politics. However, the historical approach evinced little concern either to categorize the patterns of behavior or to generalize findings beyond the bounds of particular historical events. The flow or pattern of behavior—the diplomacy of statesmen—was regarded by historians, as by the statesmen themselves, as an art and not a science. As Bismarck, one of history's most noted statesmen, once wrote:

> Politics is less a science than an art. It is not a subject which can be taught. One must have the talent for it. Even the best advice is of no avail if improperly carried out. Politics is not in itself an exact logical science, but the capacity to choose in each fleeting moment of the situation that which is least harmful or most opportune.[1]

The diplomatic historians' objective was to make the behavior of the Bismarcks, Talleyrands, Richelieus, and Metternichs comprehensible. While the actions of these statesmen might be made understandable, the lessons learned were not applied to other contexts.

SOCIAL SCIENCE APPROACHES

Those employing historical approaches were unwilling or unable to investigate the general patterns of influence—to search for a wider logic and explanation. Following World War II, however, social science perspectives that advocated the systematic analysis of international relations emerged in political science. These behavioral and quantitative approaches made progress in moving international relations from a solely descriptive discipline to a more consciously theoretic one. More rigorous definitions of key international relations terms were created, hypotheses relating these concepts were suggested, and in many cases data were collected to test these hypotheses.[2] Furthermore, quantitative international relations brought sophisticated statistical techniques to the examination of international politics.

Yet the various social science approaches, both theoretic and methodological, have not always aided the general effort to explain international relations outcomes. And, of particular concern here, they seriously inhibited the examination of diplomacy.

Systems theory. Early behavioral research in international relations theory (Kaplan, 1957; McClelland, 1966; Rosecrance, 1963) turned to a systems-theory approach to describe and explain the international system. A "systems approach" appeared to provide a level of analysis that was both comprehensive and broad enough to further scientific efforts. But the definition of a system was difficult if not impossible to arrive at for international relations. Indeed, rather than proving comprehensive, this approach was found to be too vague and amorphous. Moreover, the system proved too abstract a level of analysis: systems analysis proved too static for changeable nation-state activity. As a consequence, the systems approach was unable to explain the greater portion of interstate behavior.

Quantitative aggregate-data analysis. With the systems approach achieving only limited results, analysts turned to the level of analysis at the other end of the continuum—the individual actor. This "actor-analysis" approach focused primarily on a state's characteristics or attributes as a means to explain interstate behavior.[3] The earliest quantitative approaches emphasized the links between international and national characteristics of the actors and outcomes. Broadly, the aggregate-data approach concentrated on "the background conditions that might reasonably covary with war" (Singer, 1976: 28). The behavioral variables—so central to earlier diplomatic history—because but a second set of variables, representing "*actions* and *interactions* by which nations and other international actors 'convert' background conditions into many disputes, some crises and occasional wars" (Singer, 1976: 28). Aggregate-data approaches contended that the greater portion of explanation lay in the system's structure—its power distributions, status, or alliances, or in differences in the domestic structures, including ideology, political institutions, or rates and intensity of domestic conflict.

Yet the findings revealed (Singer, 1963; Russett, 1972; Rummel, 1972; Rosecrance et al., 1974) that only a limited part of a state's behavior could be determined by its attributes. The links between attributes and behavior are not consistent. This and other shortcomings of the quantitative-attribute approaches emerge in a short review of some of the major quantitative projects.

THE CORRELATES OF WAR

One of the chief difficulties of the Correlates of War project centered on its universality, both in its theoretic conception and its statistical techniques. It focused on the onset of war as defined by the project, lumping together all the varied instances of military conflict. This method obscured key distinctions in international relations. While the efforts of Singer and Small and their associates[4] was premised on the use of actual historical fact, the manner of analysis became, in fact, ahistorical. Furthermore, the broad correlational approaches proved limited for purposes of analysis. In one key early piece, for instance, while examining the relationship of alliance aggregation to the onset of war, Singer and Small (1966) discovered a relationship of - .29 between alliance aggregation and the onset of war in the nineteenth century, and a relationship of + .26 between alliance aggregation and the onset of war in the twentieth. Precisely because of this generalized statistical approach, little could be learned from such findings. The correlational methods effectively prevented an adequate temporal relationship between the independent and dependent variables. Many data points had to be included for significance purposes; the results gave no clues as to whether the alliances of some actors (as opposed to others) were significantly related to the onset of war.

In more recent efforts (Gochman, 1980) there have been attempts to move away from this focus on very broad findings, identifying instead key actors. But the data remain relatively abstract, atemporal, and without context, leaving the analyst with little to state other than to outline the variations in the relationship of the variables.

Another key problem revealed by the COW project was a narrow definition of the nature of diplomacy. For this project, initially, the behavioral variable was the extent of war or the intensity of war in the system only. Thus, the broad range of interactions between states was excluded in a rather single-minded attention to war. Even in the extension of the range of the dependent variable (Levy, 1977; Wallace, 1979; Gochman 1980) to include serious disputes, the analysis focused on conflict alone.

THE DIMENSIONALITY OF NATIONS

Like the Correlates of War, the Dimensionality of Nations project centered on conflict behavior and the structural explanations of conflict. In the project's early work, only foreign conflict behavior was assembled for the wide range of states identified for examination. In its initial analysis it began an extensive effort to identify the major attributes that explained interstate conflict behavior for the contemporary states from 1955 to 1957 (Rummel, 1968). The theoretic explanation linking attributes and conflict behavior derived from Quincy Wright's (1942) work on field theory in international relations. Field theory presented a spatial approach in which states of the international system were located in time-space coordinates of geographic, value, and capability dimensions. In such a view, each state could be described as lying within a multidimensional field of attributes. In the original research (Rummel, 1963, 1964, 1968, 1972) Rummel reported, however, that there was no systematic relationship between attributes and behavior. The further efforts of Tanter (1966), Wilkenfeld (1968, 1969), and Zinnes (1972) either supported the negative findings or provided only partial support without offering significant further conclusions.

Though the DON project evolved beyond field theory to social-field theory and then status-field theory, this change also signaled a shift to a much narrower interpretation of the model. In the more mature model each dyad's interactions were uniquely and empirically defined.[5] It remained unclear how generalizable the theory really was.

THE STANFORD PROJECT

The Stanford Project (The Stanford Studies in International Conflict and Integration), like many of the projects already mentioned, evolved through several distinct research stages. The initial stage closely focused on decisions. A second stage turned in a more structural direction.

The early research focused on a very short period of decision making—the six weeks before the onset of World War One (Holsti, 1972; Holsti et al., 1968; Zinnes, 1968; Zinnes et al., 1972). Like many projects, its examination was temporally narrow and focused exclusively on a crisis environment. The wider patterns of behavior were ignored, and the scale used was defined by the types of cooperation found in this particular period (Moses et al., 1967). One unique feature of the Project was its focus on perceptions and attitudes. Its framework of analysis became a two-step mediated stimulus-response model. This model provided two intervening perceptual categories—(r), the perception by the national decision system of its situation given the other actor's behavior, and (s), the actor's expressions of its own intentions, plans, actions, or attitude toward another actor (Holsti et al., 1968: 33). This perceptual framework, however, suffered from certain significant shortcomings. The requirements of a systematic perceptual analysis were quite high. The effort to code the perceptions of actors for these six weeks took years of work. More important, the juxtaposition of behaviors and attitudes within essentially the same source made it impossible to extract a behavior universe as complex as the attitude universe. Thus, behavior was reduced to attributes such as mobilization rates or gold flows.[6] So, while perceptions could be very sensitively measured, behavior now was a far cruder operational concept.

The temporal and conceptual narrowness of the Project led some of its principal researchers to rethink the theoretic thrust of the Project. They themselves recognized the possibly idio-syncratic nature of the original research. As Choucri and North (1972: 81) stated: "A crisis, however, is only the small tip of an obscured iceberg of competitions, antagonisms, relatively non-violent conflicts, arms races, and previous crisis." Their response was the conceptualization of "lateral pressure" (Choucri and North, 1975; North, 1977). In this expanded perspective, which included an empirical examination of the period from 1870 to 1914, they developed a complex model linking demographic growth, technological development, to resource demands by nations and to the external consequences of those demands. This new view points up all the limitations of structural perspec-tives. The model hypothesized a direct, though complex, rela-tionship between conceptually and temporally distinct structural variables and foreign conflict behavior. Though the method-ology was extremely sophisticated the results were limited: The various countries examined did not fit the lateral pressure model well (especially Austria-Hungary). It led North (1977) to move to an almost ideal-type analysis of state conflict behavior varying just the three principal variables—population, tech-nology, and access to resources.

Thus, the methods chosen by quantitative aggregate-data analyses to investigate outcomes in international relations have resulted in broad indiscriminate findings; as in the case of systems analysis, where the level of inquiry proved too general for a better understanding of international relations. In addition, aggregate-data analyses focused primarily on the structural characteristics, relegating behavior to a secondary position. When these projects did focus on behavior it was on war, crisis, or conflict; they ignored the broader dimensions of behavior. These projects, in fact, largely ignored the role of diplomacy in trying to explain outcomes in international relations. And they found it necessary (because of methodological restrictions) to ignore temporal elements of explanation.

Still, the systems and actor approaches represented only a part of the larger social science effort to explain outcomes. A further approach focused on "actor interaction."[7] In contrast to the structural approaches of actor analysis, actor interaction placed the influence of behavior "front and center" in trying to explain outcomes in international politics. Placing behavior in a more central position also failed to solve all the problems related to an examination of the patterns of diplomacy.

Strategy and social psychology. Strategy and game theory were approaches enthusiastically welcomed by political scientists studying interaction among states. Game theory, particularly, appeared to provide a new tool potentially powerful enough to explain interstate bargaining. It is interesting that the matrix of the two-person game, the most frequent version of game theory in international relations, dovetailed well with the political reality of East-West tensions and superpower bipolarity. Even the assumptions of underlying conflicts of interest between players appeared consistent with the nature of the Cold War. In a world where force, nuclear deterrence, and retaliation had become the perceived means of maintaining the balance of power in the international system, the stress on "rational decisions in conflict situations" (Rapoport et al., 1976: 3) seemed appropriate. If the pure conflict (zero-sum games) appeared too extreme, then mixed-motive games, Chicken and Prisoner's Dilemma (Snyder, 1961; Lockhart, 1973; Jervis, 1972), for example, seemed to capture well the strategies and outcomes of the then, contemporary environment.

Even with the employment of mixed-motive games, the assumptions of game theory posed serious problems to the examination of interstate behavior. Notions of perfect information between players, simultaneous moves with no communication certainly failed to match the international system. Also, the single-game format was unrealistic in international politics, where bargaining between actors represented a continuous set of interactions. In other words, game theory as originally described was not appropriate to real-world situations.

However, social psychology, another social science discipline, provided political scientists with a laboratory setting, a place to test hypotheses about strategy and bargaining. Social psychologists had long been interested in small group behavior. They recognized, as Rapoport (1960: 224-225) pointed out, that "classical game theory is *not* based on experimental evidence. It represents an attempt to build normative theory on a foundation of *strategic logic.*" Thus, social psychologists plunged into experimentation—based often on particular games, such as Prisoner's Dilemma—with the intent of determining the efficacy of types of behavior on particular outcomes; they went beyond single-play games, and they varied the restrictions on communication. In the end, many findings from these experiments were presented for their possible insight into behavior and interaction.

But limitations existed here as well. The simulation of a bargaining environment in the laboratory compatible with international relations seemed dubious: the face-to-face laboratory world remained far from most international situations; the attitudes and motivations of players in experimental games were unlikely to match attitudes and motivations of those making decisions in international politics. The focus on conflict remained. Though social psychologists were interested in both cooperation and conflict, conflict research predominated (Kelman, 1965; Deutsch, 1973).

Yet further game-theoretic research efforts continue with the aim of greater realism in bargaining games. In a new approach, Axelrod (1980) tested Prisoner's Dilemma with specialists in the field instead of unknown volunteers. This experiment contrasted sharply with earlier laboratory experiments, yet it only reinforced the view that the role of cooperation has been underestimated in much of the previous work on strategy and bargaining. Unfortunately, it did not solve the problem associated with use of an artificial environment and its consequent applicability to international relations.

Besides this new experimental approach, a more historical approach was applied by Snyder and Diesing (1977) and Lockhard (1977, 1979). In their studies, various international crises were defined by mixed-motive strategies. But "fitting history" to these simplifying strategies both altered the logic of strategies such as the classic Prisoner's Dilemma and left open to debate the choices of the strategies by the authors for the complex historical cases. Finally, as with many other approaches, these analysts focused soely on conflict or the crises of the international system isolated from the wider patterns of diplomacy.

Events-data analysis. Fortunately, not all analysis of the interaction between states depends on game theory and bargaining. A unique approach to actor interaction was developed by the events-data movement. This method turned directly to the concerns of diplomatic historians–the actions and interactions of nation-states. Events-data research accepted that the behavior of statesmen was of crucial interest to international outcomes and analyzed the real historical record of Great Power interactions. In contrast to the diplomatic historians. Events researchers were unwilling to remain content with detailed descriptions of the interactions of the powers. Instead, events-data projects categorized behavior in various ways and then tested hypotheses with these more strictly defined actions. In effect, the events-data approach applied social science criteria and methods to the data of diplomatic historians assuming "that events data collectors were tapping the major political acts and decisions of international actors" (Peterson, 1975: 264).

Thus, events research offered social science rigor to the analysis of diplomacy. Yet those employing an events-data approach were not immune to the problems that had plagued researchers in structural aggregate-data projects, and there were unique problems to cope with in events-data approaches as well. As in earlier quantitative studies, events data researchers collected events on all countries of the international system without distinguishing between them in terms of importance. Far worse was the emphasis on data collection to the detriment of theory. There was little or no attention given to developing a theory of relevant propositions concerning interaction. The work of Charles McClelland, a pioneer in events-data research, reveals some of the strengths and weaknesses of the early events-data analysis. McClelland (1961, 1962, 1968, 1972) developed a large events-data collection called the World Event/Interaction Survey (WEIS). Applying coding and scaling techniques to the *New York Times,* this project extracted the flow of actions from one nation to another beginning in 1966. But, like aggregate-data research, the focus of interest quickly became crisis. Furthermore, the WEIS analyses were primarily comparative pictures of the patterns of actions in various crises without explicit hypotheses on interaction.

Whatever the limitations, however, McClelland's efforts cleared the way for further events-data projects. While these projects too suffered from various shortcomings, the systematic analysis of real state actions opened the events-data movement and provided the means to test real-world interaction—to discover the logic of diplomacy, as we shall see.

THE BEHAVIORAL CORRELATES OF WAR

The Behavioral Correlates of War Project was a spin-off from the original Correlates of War project. However, unlike the original COW project, this new one focused primarily on behavior as an explanation of international relations outcomes. In order to examine interstate actions, BCOW, as it came to be called, developed a typology of international behavior (Leng and Singer, 1970; Leng, 1972) and a rigorous means of coding and classifying. Though initially focused on crisis patterns (Leng and Goodsell, 1974), much like earlier events data analyses, BCOW developed hypotheses and tested actual patterns of interaction between states (Leng and Wheeler, 1979; Leng 1980). BCOW can then be seen as an evolution of the original Correlates of War from solely structural explanations to behavioral ones, and from broad patterns of behavior to actual patterns of interaction.

BCOW retains many of the perspectives of the original project. While a wider view of behavior is now available with BCOW, the focus of this project is still on crises isolated from the broader patterns of diplomacy. In addition, the logic of the statistical testing still closely defines how interaction is conceptualized. As a result, a potpourri of actors and crises are included in their broad tests. For instance, Leng (1980: 132) includes dyadic cases encompassing the Poles and Czechoslovakians, the Bolivians and Paraguayans, and the British and the Portuguese. The tendency is once again to ignore the context, to use historical data ahistorically: History becomes little more than data points without the continuity provided by context.

DON AND CREON

Though the Dimensionality of Nations Project, as mentioned earlier, focused on structural explanations of conflict, there were analysts who used its data for research on interaction. Warren Phillips (1971), for instance, employing data from DON, attempted to test the hypothesis that a state's conflict behavior was related the conflict actions and responses of states. His tests of interaction revealed yet another problem in the events-data movement—the logic of aggregation. Phillips looked at the actions of one state toward the environment and the responses of the environment to those actions. The test was incapable of matching the responses of particular nations to the actions of others. Phillips could only show that the levels of conflict received and sent by an actor to all actors and received from all actors to an actor were strongly related: The broad quantitative approach obscured any significant relationships between powers.

Aware of some of these limitations, Phillips shifted to a dyadic level of analysis in later studies (Phillips and Crain, 1974) and used data gathered by the Comparative Research on the Events of Nations project (CREON).

CREON is a comparative foreign policy analysis project, as the title suggests. In a systematic way the project has attempted to define comparatively the sources of foreign policy decisions. Hypotheses have been constructed and tested (East et al., 1978) which relate decision structure and decision process to particular foreign policy behavior.

Phillips and Crain (1974), using CREON, touched more on interaction than has been the case since. CREON provided a data base which at least included cooperative as well as conflictual actors, improving on the DON data. Yet the "logic of aggregation" still defeated their efforts to examine interaction, even after they had put their research on a dyadic basis. The analysis still failed to define the patterns of action and response, instead of doing so, Phillips and Crain aggregated the data into types of behavior and correlated those aggregations. Once again they ignored the actual patterns of interactions among states.

THE SITUATIONAL ANALYSIS PROJECT

From its inception, the Situational Analysis Project possessed the capacity to test seriously actor-interaction approaches, though it did not do so, as we shall see. Like many events projects, its early research was focused on structural hypotheses (Rosecrance et al., 1974), though with a more highly developed dependent (behavioral) variable. And, like other events projects, it did not escape methodological limitations (particularly aggregation) when it did come to focus on interaction. Jeffrey Hart (1974) employed a portion of SAP's data to test actor interaction—specifically symmetry. Using data that was both conflictual and cooperative, Hart hoped to show that a nation that was cooperative would receive cooperation and that a nation that acted conflictually would receive conflictual action. However, just as with Phillips (1971, 1973) and Phillips and Crain (1974),

Hart's research strategy made it impossible truly to test inter-action. Though he paired the powers, Hart aggregated the scored behavior over yearly periods. This aggregation destroyed the possibility of any test of discrete interactions. Hart could not test symmetry either: it was impossible from the measure-ment of behavior over a year to determine if a simple positive or negative action resulted in particular positive or negative re-sponses. The analysis was very disappointing.

With all the mistakes and shortcomings of the events-data movement, its emergence, nevertheless, was an important step in providing a means to examine the diplomacy of the powers in a systematic way. Events data focused on behavior. Unlike game theory and social psychology, approaches that had initially investigated interaction, events data turned to the real actions of statesmen. Moreover, of all the projects examined, the Situ-ational Analysis Project, because of its unique characteristics (which will be described more fully in the next section), pro-vided an ideal means to seek to uncover the logic of diplomacy.

THE DATA BASE AND THE FRAMEWORK OF ANALYSIS

It was essential to find a means to test systematically the real diplomacy of states without giving up the sensitivity to indi-vidual country actions or historical context. The SAP project proved ideal for these requirements. The events analyzed were those culled from diplomatic histories. The project was seen by its director, Professor Richard Rosecrance, as a means to accomplish "systemic history" (Rosecrance et al., 1969: ·54). For testing, the actions of the European powers from 1870 to 1890 were categorized and measured.[8] While the project abstracted those events of international politics of the powers—Great Britain, France, Russia, Prussia/Germany, Austria-Hungary, and Italy—it did so recognizing the comparative and holistic character of international politics. It did not abstract the actions of a particular dyad for the period but of all the major actors, offering an opportunity to assess fully the effects of the actions of each country toward all others and in various contexts. The period chosen—1870 to 1890—was one rich in varied diplomatic settings. In these twenty-one years, there were several conflicts (the Franco-Prussian War in 1870-71 and the Russo-Turkish War in 1877-78); there were crises (the "War-in-Sight" crisis and two occurrences of Balkan tension); in addition, there were periods of entente between some of the powers (as between Germany and France in the 1880s and amity between the cosigners of the Mediterranean agreements); finally, there were frequent alliances between these powers and several conferences over the Balkans and colonial issues involving most of the powers. This period is noted for the operation of various international relations mechanisms, such as the balance of power and use of alliances. Because of the use of these international techniques, this period is an important test of both the patterns of diplomacy, and of structural characteristics—power, alliance, and status. While the analysis will be limited historically and the conclusions reflect the limitations of the time period chosen, it remains a period whose implications are relevant to most of the modern state system.

In the 21 years of interactions among these European powers, more than 2000 events were coded by the Situational Analysis Project, yielding some 5280 interactions. Each interaction coded the actor, the target or targets, and a measurement of the degree of cooperativeness of the action.[9] Several possible frameworks from the literature appeared to be capable of appropriately testing interaction. We chose one that focused on behavior and would truly include a test of symmetry. This stimulus framework response had the advantages of being concerned directly with behavior and of focusing on the influence of actions between states A and B.

As we pointed out earlier, the employment of this framework by analysts is far from universal. The Stanford Project employed a two-step mediated stimulus-response model. The emphasis in this framework (S-r: s-R) is on attitudes and perceptions. Such a framework, as we mentioned, limits the sensitivity to the actual behavioral interaction. In addition, there are other influence frameworks that are tuned to the perceptual and cognitive elements (Singer, 1963; Axelrod, 1976). Rich in detail about the decision-making processes, these frameworks require credible descriptions of decision makers. As Robert Jervis (1970, 1976), a theorist well acquainted with perceptual analysis, has admitted, "there is no easy way to determine the accuracy of perceptions. It is hard to know what a person's perceptions were and even harder to know whether they were correct" (Jervis, 1976: 7). It is difficult to predict accurately when psychological variables will influence the actions of states. For example, attitudes are dispositional; present attitudes may not invariably influence behavior. How and when attitudes influence behavior remains unclear.

In this analysis we are primarily interested in behavior. A mediated stimulus-response model would require us to employ too crude a definition of behavior for an adequate examination of diplomatic behavior. Furthermore, the difficulty of coding psychological variables and of suggesting the relationship of these variables to behavior points up the advantages of subsuming perceptions and attitudes into behavior. With behavioral interaction examined, further analysis employing attitudinal and perceptual variables is always possible, though we shall not attempt such an analysis here.

In their directed-dyad form, the Situational Analysis Project's data are well suited for a stimulus-response analysis. Nevertheless, the data, as originally collected and scaled, were not useful immediately to analysis within this framework. To make the data useful for a symmetry test, it was necessary to reanalyze all of the cases, extracting interactions in a stimulus-response manner for our six powers. Of the 5280 interactions, only 3183 cases of actions involved any two of our six powers. However, not all of these can be included in a stimulus-response framework. As Jeffrey Hart (1974: 231) pointed out in his work on the Situational Analysis Project, many actions are symbolic and not particularly influence oriented; these cases would not be extracted for use in a stimulus-response examination. Furthermore, in some cases actions induce no immediate response. Cases of no response form a separate subset of all stimulus-response cases.

In the end, some 1433 action-response and action-no response interactions were identified. In extracting these cases, a set of coding rules governed the procedure in order to enhance consistency and reliability. The coding rules included:

(1) In general, only directed behavioral interactions were used. Indirect influences were ignored unless the original action stimulated a response from an indirect target.

(2) There were cases of proposals to meet or negotiate and actions that announced the commencement of negotiations or the start of a meeting. While the proposal would be extracted, the follow-on event would be omitted.

(3) Multilateral actions were broken down into discrete dyads. In events where individual powers were not mentioned—cases where it was simply all powers to all powers—the event was omitted for its vagueness.

(4) As pointed out earlier, all symbolic actions were excluded; therefore, events like head-of-state trips or the beginnings of meetings were omitted.

(5) All agreements and alliances, because they were nondirectional (reciprocal), were coded for both states.

In order to assure the consistency and reliability of these rules, after a sufficient delay, some portions of the data were reexamined. It was found that the intercoder reliability with the previous examination came to .90. This reliability level assured a generally consistent data set within the limitations of the research.

Coding interaction was a key to examining the patterns of diplomacy. Previous aggregative techniques had ignored that key element of interaction—identifying actions which are stimuli and actions which are responses. In projects which did not ignore the interaction question, notably the Stanford Project, the solution was to identify all stimuli as responses as well. But precisely because the Situational Analysis Project maintained the chronology and context of actions of all the powers, such a solution was not required here in preparing to test symmetry. The Project's coded events were detailed enough to enable us to pair actions and their responses individually.

In addition, the coding of the events by the Situational Analysis Project provided a convenient and rigorous means to test the basic but crucial pattern of interaction—symmetry. The Project scales all actions along a conflict-cooperation continuum; the interval scale employed in this research identifies thirty-two categories of events. The scale itself is divided at 50, which is regarded as informational and neutral between the cooperative actions, measured from 50 to 100, and conflictual actions, measured from 50 to 1. Though the scale is a continuum suggesting a single dimension, there are, in fact, two broad categories of events—one conflictual and the other cooperative. Employing the notion that our actions can be grouped together as either cooperative actions or conflictual actions, we defined the symmetry of behavior by the identity of valence or sign. Conflictual actions (those for 50 to 1) were defined positively (+). Thus, the symmetry of our interactions in our stimulus-response framework can be defined simply as positive action (+) and a postive response (+), or negative action (-) and a negative response (-).

INVESTIGATING BEHAVIOR AND STRUCTURE

The Situational Analysis Project provided the means to examine the influence of diplomacy on the outcomes of international relations. The historians afford us valuable insights into the course of the diplomacy of these six European powers, but provide no evidence of the possible underlying patterns of diplomatic influence. However, the Situational Analysis Project incorporated the Symmetry Hypothesis, extending our understanding of the historical record by testing for the symmetry of cooperative and conflictual actions.

In this critique of the international relations literature and description of the techniques employed in this project, we have shown both the need and a means to put the primary focus on behavior, specifically, interaction. Behavior is at the core of our systematic testing of outcomes in this period. Having accomplished this, however, we want to turn our attention to the mechanisms and the structures of international relations. How do we combine structural explanations, so frequently cited in the literature, with an interaction approach such as the one presented here? Our analysis is not only a sweeping test of symmetry over a period of two decades. We wish to explain the patterns of diplomacy over time; we want to explain the differences in the patterns of symmetry between the various powers.

Structural variables, then, can be seen as a key addition to the core explanation of the patterns of diplomacy and the outcomes of international relations. In order to test structural variables, we begin with the differences in the level of symmetry and our first structural variable—power. Power traditionally has been used to explain international relations behavior. It has been argued that both the balance of power and the imbalance of power determine cooperation and conflict outcomes in the international system. Indeed, power (or capability) differences have dominated "actor analysis" approaches to quantitative international relations. If a structural explanation holds, we would expect to find that power difference should explain the differences in the levels of symmetric interaction—both co-operative and conflictual. Our Power Hypothesis argues that the more equal the power between our actors, the more symmetric their interactions; and the more unequal the power between our actors, the less symmetric their interactions.[10]

The same logic used with the analysis of symmetry applies to our power examination. Our historical description describes fully over these years the differences in power among our actors. Because power is such a protean concept, the analysis develops as broad a description of power as possible. Military power, resource power, and industrial power are all included; the strengths and weaknesses of the six European countries are described in detail. But once again, the historical description suggests no patterns. Only by suggesting the Power Hypothesis can we test the relationship between the many power differences and the diplomatic patterns. Finally, our general negative findings can be related to pairs of countries that display patterns of interaction symmetry that disconfirm the Power Hypothesis.

Alliance and status are other structural characteristics that have been used to explain behavioral outcomes in international relations. Alliances are closely associated with power in traditional balance of power explanations. The presence of alliances has been argued both to cause conflict and to reduce its likelihood in the international system. Status and status inconsistency also have been closely identified with cooperative and conflictual behavior in international relations.

The Alliance Hypothesis argues that the stronger the alliance ties between the actors, the lower their levels both cooperative and conflictual of symmetry, while the weaker the alliance ties between the actors, the higher their levels of symmetry.

Status differences suggest two hypotheses. The first—the Cooperative Hypothesis—suggests that the higher the joint status of two actors, the higher the level of cooperative symmetry and the lower the level of conflictual symmetry. The lower the joint status of two actors, the lower the level of cooperative symmetry and the higher the level of conflictual symmetry. Our other status hypothesis—the Status Inconsistency Hypothesis—focuses more on status inconsistency and argues that the greater the status inconsistency between actors, the higher the levels of conflictual symmetry and the lower levels of cooperative symmetry. The lower the status inconsistency between actors, the higher the cooperative symmetry and the lower conflictual symmetry.

Our tests of alliance and status with symmetry, as with power and symmetry, are made more effective both by detailed descriptions of alliance and status differences, and by the ability to follow up our general tests with discrete analyses of the pairs of countries. But as with power, neither alliance nor status is sensitive enough to the changes in symmetry over time and across all our powers. The "discrete analysis" techniques reveal the limitations of the initial structural hypotheses. Overall, this extensive historical and quantitative approach seriously undermines traditional explanations and supports hypotheses emphasizing the importance of diplomacy and more diplomatically defined structural characteristics. The discrete analysis brings us right back to the historian's concern—diplomacy. It accomplishes this' task by employing a social science concern for general patterns and broader explanations. As a result, the study begins with the diplomacy of the European powers in the Bismarckian system and ends with the logic of diplomacy.

NOTES

1. Cited in Pflanze (1976: 161-162) from *Bismarck: Die Gesammelten Werke* (Berlin, 1924-1935) IX, 399.

2. J. David Singer (1969, 1974) was particularly important in urging analysts to collect data for testing international relations theory. One of the main contributions of the Correlates of War Project, his project, was to encourage the collection of evidence for the testing of theory in international relations.

3. We should make clear, however, that frequently in this approach it was a systemic view that was being tested. This apparent contradiction resulted from the fact that analysts would aggregate capabilities for all actors, for instance, or aggregate the alliances for all actors and compare them over time. The tests, while systemic, were also reductionist.

4. The findings from the Correlates of War Project are substantial. For a full accounting of the research, see Hoole and Zinnes (1976: 481-488) and Singer (1960: 323-328).

5. The early model was defined in the following way:

$$w_{i \to j,k} = \sum_{\ell=1}^{P} a_\ell d_{i-j,\ell}$$

where the behavior of a dyad i– was the weighted force vector d (attributes distances). This first model was found to explain behavior poorly. As a result, some of the assumptions of the model were questioned. In particular, the view that the behavior of each is exactly determined by the same forces was cited as an overly restrictive condition of Model I. In order to avoid this assumption and the corresponding one that behavior of state i to j was exactly equal to the behavior of j to i, a second model (Model II) was defined:

$$w_{i \to j,k} = \sum_{\ell=1}^{P} a_{i\ell} d_{i-j,\ell}$$

It was from this model defining less generally the attribute distances on behavior that status field theory evolved.

6. Gordon Hilton (1970: 129), reviewing the entire project, suggested that its limited findings "might be due to the action data. There is little reason to suppose

that mobilisations were the only stimuli which produced perceptions of hostility. . . . It may be the case that no action data, collected haphazardly, will give good results when processed with the rigorously collected perceptual data."

7. In reviewing various approaches to international relations recently, Michael Sullivan (1976: 255-256) described this approach in the following way: "One type of analytical system that can be treated is the system of interactions made up of the behavior of states toward one another. Natural leaders, in other words, do not act completely independently; they know that their actions are likely to produce counteractions by other leaders. . . . Nations therefore often become 'locked in' to other nations through their interactions, and that fact alone has a bearing on their behavior."

8. For a detailed analysis of the methods employed in developing the events data of the situational Analysis Project, see Goodman et al. (1975).

9. The Situational Analysis Project accepted the perspective that interstate behaviors could be placed along a continuum of cooperation and conflict. In order to create a relatively exhaustive typology of events (verbal and nonverbal, conflictual and cooperative), an initial list of forty-two categories was developed by synthesizing and generalizing three previously developed typologies. Dissatisfied with a typology of events solely, Richard Rosecrance, the director, undertook to measure, quantitatively, the degree of cooperation or conflict each category exhibited. As a result, several researchers ranked all the event categories by degree of cooperation and conflict: from this effort a full thirty-two-category interval scale of interstate behavior with a high degree of reliability was created (Goodman et al., 1975: 46-50). The final product—the Corkeley scale—provided researchers with a sensitive measuring instrument for differentiating the actions and interactions of the statesmen.

10. In this analysis of the relationship of structural variables to symmetry, we consciously employ techniques which enable us to combine our general hypothesis testing with the confirmation of history. In order to avoid the "systemic fallacy"— the inability to examine evidence below the system level because of statistical methods—we employ discrete paired-comparison and qualitative techniques. This approach allows us to test all the interaction patterns of our powers and still allows us to refer back to particular pairs of powers to suggest why the historical record either supports or denies the hypothesis. For a detailed description of the techniques used in this analysis, see the Methodology Appendix.

120751

Chapter 3

THE DIPLOMACY OF THE EUROPEAN POWERS, 1870 TO 1890

THE EVENTS OF 1870-1890

The complexity of diplomatic interactions is amply demonstrated in any description of the two decades of international politics of the late nineteenth century. Diplomatic historians (Fay, 1930; Langer, 1950; Schmitt, 1934; Sontag, 1933; Taylor, 1954) have analyzed the motivations, events, and interactions of the Great Powers of these years. Their scholarly efforts have outlined the importance of the European diplomats and statesmen in influencing the outcomes of this international system. However, their efforts have failed to provide an understanding of the patterns of diplomatic interactions.

The following chapter summarizes the diplomatic interactions of the powers of these years, drawing on these rich diplomatic sources. This summary focuses on the cooperative and conflictual patterns of the European powers. However, the historical tradition illustrates the limitations of this approach for patterns of cooperation and conflict.

The diplomacy of the powers of these two decades begins in conflict. The Franco-Prussian War (1870-1871) shattered the temporary calm established in Europe following the conflict of 1866. It also heralded the end of an era in international relations. For after the crowning of William I as German Emperor, Central Europe would never again see a vacuum of power in central Europe. The crowning in the Hall of Mirrors at Versailles also resolved, if only temporarily, the German national question. Yet nationalities were a constant irritant in this new international system, and the settlement of this war added another dimension to them, one that would poison European politics right down to the World War I. The loss of Alsace and part of Lorraine—in the Treaty of Frankfort—was seized on by French nationalists in the succeeding decades as a symbol of national disgrace. It would prove an insurmountable obstacle to the permanent improvement of Franco-German relations.

The loss of Alsace and Lorraine was not, however, the only national question facing European diplomats after 1871. Further east, the Balkans came alive with political ferment. Balkan instability became directly important to the wider international system because of the roles of the two aging empires—Austria-Hungary and the Ottoman Empire. This agitation for independence among Balkan groups led the Ottoman Turks into a series of wars that ended, finally, in Turkey's eviction from most of Europe. For Austria-Hungary, which, except for Russia, remained the last multinational state in Europe, the breakup of the Ottoman Empire created both internal and external tensions. Domestically, the growing list of independent states prompted secessionist or autonomist movements among similar ethnic groups inside the Empire. Internationally, Austria-Hungary faced a growing Russian interest in the Balkans. As a result, the 1870s and 1880s were witness to a growing rivalry between these two European powers for control of the Balkans.

As if these major areas of nationalist conflict were not sufficient, international relations were further strained by the final Great Power scramble for colonies. The final division of Africa and Asia among the Great Powers (excluding Austria-Hungary) increased tensions and multiplied quarrels throughout the international system. From Egypt to Indochina and Afghanistan to southwest Africa, the clash of national interests of the European powers raged.

In the history of diplomacy, the period from 1870 to 1890 is best known for the central importance of the new German Empire and its first chancellor—Otto von Bismarck. This newly consolidated Germany and its indomitable Chancellor insured that Germany's concerns became vital European concerns. As a result, French revanchism became emmeshed in wider diplomatic actions. The Balkan problems, serious enough in themselves, were exacerbated by Bismarck's need to create an alignment of powers large and powerful enough to forestall French aggression. Furthermore, German attitudes on colonial issues came to be seen in light of the larger question of the alignment of the powers.

These twenty-one years of international relations, in fact, can be organized effectively by three issue areas—the alignment of forces by Germany, conflicts in the Balkans, and colonial disputes. While almost all participated in every issue, Germany's role was paramount. The appearance of a strong state in Central Europe transformed European politics. This factor, as well as Bismarckian predominance in diplomatic circles, argues for the usefulness of such a German and Bismarckian focus.

Germany's diplomatic influence in the 1870s began with the Franco-Prussian War. Prussia's defeat of France, still regarded in 1870 as Europe's premier continental power, shocked the Great powers. French pleas for arbitration went unheeded, and, in the end, Germany imposed its own terms on a defeated and stunned France. By the standards of the time, the Frankfort Treaty was harsh. The monetary terms were regarded as particularly punitive. Yet of more immediate concern to the international politics of the 1870s was France's rapid payment of its indemnity and her evident military recovery, which caused considerable worry in the new German Empire. France's rapid renewal convinced Bismarck that further actions were necessary to keep France in check. Though confident of Germany's strength, Bismarck was concerned over the Empire's position should France gain the support of either Austria-Hungary or Russia. The forestalling of any combination of France and either alternative continental power thus became a signal requirement for the German Chancellor.

For Bismarck, one method of preventing any such combination was the maintenance of France's isolation by drawing Germany closer to both other major continental powers. Bismarck effected this with meetings between the Heads of both Russia and Austria-Hungary. The result was a set of military agreements between Germany and Russia, and Russia and Austria, collectively known as the Three Emperors' League (1873). The League emphasized the status quo and monarchical solidarity. More important, it provided Bismarck with a means of keeping France isolated from possible allies.

A military law passed by the French assembly provided Bismarck with a pretext to indicate a German willingness to meet French revanchism with force if necessary. This diplomatic episode, the "War-in-Sight" crisis (1875), named for an article published in the *Berlin Post,* dramatically increased tensions between the two countries. The article, thought to be written by government officials at the time, warned of the possibility of a German preemptive strike to forestall a French recovery which might threaten Germany's security. Though aimed at further isolating France from potential political allies, it had the opposite effect.

The French appealed to the other powers to prevent a repetition of 1870. Austria-Hungary and Italy declined to join in a demarche, but Great Britain and Russia warned Germany they would not countenance a second French defeat. Such sympathetic attitudes, particularly on the part of Russia and Britain, pleased the French, most especially the French Foreign Minister, the Duc Decazes. By adroit efforts, the French has succeeded in ending their diplomatic isolation.[1]

If the War-in-Sight crisis proved unproductive for Bismarck's policy of isolating France, events in the Balkans in the mid-1870s presaged even greater difficulties for Bismarckian diplomacy. Bismarck asserted that Germany had no direct interests in the Balkans. This was not the case for either Austria-Hungary or Russia; both of those countries were deeply involved in the disposition of the European Ottoman Empire. Thus, while Bismarck discounted any direct German interests there, his desire to align the powers of Europe favorably toward Germany (and unfavorably toward France) necessitated German participation in Great Power disputes in the Balkans.

These disputes erupted on the heels of the outbreak of insurrections in Bosnia and Herzegovina in 1875; at the time, both were territories of the Ottoman Empire. The following year, Serbia and Montenegro declared war on Turkey in hopes of territorial gain. The response of the powers was largely restricted to attempts to impose reforms on the Ottoman Turks. However, solidarity was not easy to achieve. In fact, the British, fearful of Russian designs on the Straits, opposed all the reform schemes of the powers. The lack of Great Power agreement provided Turkey with ample means to avoid accepting any proposals, while at the same time prosecuting the war against the insurgents. The failure of the powers to impose reforms on the Turks ultimately led to a series of negotiations between Russia and Austria-Hungary intended to find some acceptable solution to the Balkan crisis. The results of these negotiations, formalized in the Reichstadt agreements and the Budapest conventions (1876), fixed the conditions for Austrian neutrality in case of Russian intervention. In point of fact, these agreements provided Russia with the freedom it desired to proceed with a military solution to the Balkan crisis.

With Austrian neutrality secured, Russia attacked Turkey in April 1877. Unfortunately for the Russians, this against a country regarded as a weak military opponent begun so enthusiastically, proved to be far more costly than originally anticipated—the costly seige of Plevna revealed a less than omnipotent

Russian Army. It was not until March 3, 1878 that Russia achieved victory by the Treaty of San Stefano. Yet the success crowned in the Treaty of San Stefano by the Russians was short-lived. Great Britain, outraged by Russian advances on the Straits, threatened war; Austria-Hungary, shocked by the terms in the Treaty—which broke earlier Austrian-Russian agreements—demanded a conference of all the European powers to review the Russian-Turkish Treaty. Bismarck, especially disquieted by these tensions between Russia and Austria, accepted the Austrian demands and issued invitations to the powers to attend a conference in Berlin.

Only with much prenegotiation between Russia and Austria, and Russia and England, did the powers finally meet in Berlin in the summer of 1878. There Bismarck displayed what he described as Germany's "honest broker" role. The German Chancellor directed all his efforts toward finding some means to satisfy the demands of Russia on the one side and those of Austria-Hungary and Britain on the other. Even with prior negotiation and the guiding hand of Bismarck, the conference was difficult and conflict ridden. Disraeli, the British prime minister, threatened to quit the conference. Bismarck himself had to threaten to leave at one point to secure a final accord. At the conference's end, however, San Stefano's territorial terms, set by Russia, were altered substantially.

The Berlin Conference thus failed to resolve tensions between Bismarck's allies. Most of the powers, reflecting on Bismarck's "honest broker" activities, praised Bismark's efforts. The Russians, however, assessing the Conference's impact on their interests, condemned Bismarck for taking an obviously anti-Russian stance. Russian ministers, and even the Tsar himself, complained bitterly and openly of Germany's pro-Austrian attitudes in the negotiations. The Tsar, in a letter to Emperor William, demanded greater German attention to Russian objectives.

The Russian pique following the Berlin Conference posed exactly the sort of dilemma Bismarck had hoped to avoid. The Chancellor found himself forced, in effect, to choose sides between Russia and Austria-Hungary. Between 1878 and 1879, in a move still not even perfectly understood today, Bismarck opened negotiations with the Habsburg Empire to establish a formal alliance. Bismarck argued, in his memoirs, that it was done to prevent a possible Austro-Russian combination. Whatever the ultimate motivations, the Austro-German Dual Alliance was the outcome of these new talks. Signed on October 22, 1879, this alliance altered substantially the relationship between the three eastern monarchies; it also marked a significant change in diplomatic practice. As Bernadotte Schmitt (1934: 16) pointed out: "The alliance marks a turning-point in the history of Europe. There had often been alliances in the past, but they had usually been concluded for specific purposes and were dissolved when the aim was achieved." This first alliance was, in fact, a prelude to a series of alliances signed or influenced by Germany to keep Russia in check—that is, away from France, and attracted to Germany. The Chancellor hoped such efforts would maintain a favorable alignment of forces against France.

The initial measure of Bismarck's success in these efforts became apparent soon after the Dual Alliance's signing. The alliance, rather than pushing Russia closer to France (which might have been expected), acted instead as a signal to the Russian court of its exposed and isolated position. The outcome of this concern was a renewed Russian interest in an alliance with Austria-Hungary. This new Russian amity was formalized in June 1881, in the establishment of the Three Emperors' Alliance signed by all three eastern monarchies—Germany, Russia, and Austria-Hungary. For Bismarck, this alliance was a means to protect a favorable alignment of forces. It promised to quiet tensions in the Balkans by committing Russia and Austria-Hungary not to alter the status quo. It also reaffirmed Austria-Hungary's right to annex Bosnia and Herzegovina; in return Russia was promised support for the eventual union of Bulgaria and Eastern Roumelia. In wider international terms, both the Dual Alliance and the Three Emperors' Alliance revealed the close interdependence, particularly for Germany, between the

Balkans and the alignment of forces in Europe. This interdependence, while protected in the short term, could not be guaranteed irrevocably by these diplomatic actions.

These first agreements did not end the alliance signing. The Triple Alliance, the next major commitment, furthered links in other issue areas for Germany by tying together questions of the alignment of forces and colonial acquisition. In the first years of the 1870s, diplomatic activity between France and Italy was quarrelsome and tense; French support for the Pope, with troops and a gunboat, quickly soured relations between the two countries. Relations were further strained by France's and Italy's shared attraction to new North African possessions. In this growing competition, an Italian company secured the rights to build a railroad between Tunis and Goletta. However, it was France that obtained influence with the Bey of Tunis (Treaty of Bardo, May 1881). Italian protests to the powers went unheeded. In fact, following the Congress of Berlin, Bismarck urged France to take Tunis. But while Italy's approaches to Germany were turned aside in the 1870s and into the 1880s, Italian appeals to Austria-Hungary and Germany by 1881 gained a far more sympathetic hearing. At Bismarck's urging and after many proposals, the signing of the Triple Alliance on May 20, 1882 provided Italy with the prestige—if not the attributes—of a major power. It also secured protection for Italy against a possible attack from France. In return, Italy pledged to defend Germany in case of a French attack, while Austria-Hungary saw in the treaty the possibility of modifying or ending Italian irredentist claims against Austrian territory. Yet behind the German encouragement and the prodding of a reticent Austria-Hungary was Bismarck's desire to align the forces of Europe securely against the French.

Colonial tensions did not end for the French with the Italian imbroglio over Tunis. More serious than Italian pique over Tunis and Tripolitania was the growing colonial tension between France and Great Britain in Egypt. Both Britain and France protected investments in Egypt; through a dual commission the two colonial powers controlled the Egyptian debt service. Their privileged position in Egypt became threatened by nationalist agitation that broke out against the Khedive in 1881. The inability of Egyptian authorities to control antiwestern agitation prompted both powers to demonstrate their support for the Khedive with a joint show of naval forces in late May. Rioting in Alexandria in June which killed fifty Europeans, convinced the British that further measures were required. On July 11, Admiral Sir Beauchamp Seymour, commanding British forces, bombarded Alexandria from the sea. Soon after this bombardment British troops were landed. The French government refused to countenance such overt actions and demonstrated its opposition by withdrawing its forces from Egypt in protest. This British landing began an occupation that would last until after World War II. It immediately exacerbated tensions between the two great imperial powers which would plague their relations for the remainder of the decade.

British-French tensions over colonial issues provided Bismarck with an opportunity to press a policy of conciliation with France. Earlier, the failure of the "War-in-Sight" crisis had marked a turning point in the Bismarckian strategy toward France. At the Berlin Congress, Bismarck went out of his way to cooperate with the French delegation (Mitchell, 1935: 87). The Chancellor made it clear to the French that they could count on German support regarding Tunis. At about the same time that Bismarck urged French action in Tunis, he counseled the British to take Egypt. By the time of the riots in Alexandria, and the widening Anglo-French rift, the Chancellor indicated growing support for France's opposition to British military initiatives.

Indeed, Bismarck set out to cooperate closely with France in a series of conferences called to deal with colonial issues in the 1880s. In the London Conference, held during the summer of 1884, and called by Britain to reorganize Egyptian finances, Bismarck's support of Jules Ferry defeated British efforts to obtain sole control over Egypt's debt service. Later, in November, at the Berlin Conference arranged by Bismarck and Ferry, the two governments worked together closely to secure the agreement of the fourteen nations participating on issues of slavery, freedom of navigation, and the rights of the powers in the Congo.

Meanwhile, for the first time Germany asserted its own claims to colonial territory. This dramatic policy shift for Bismarck inevitably led to conflicts with Great Britain, whose often undefined control of territories in southwest Africa, East Africa, Fiji, and New Guinea was challenged by Germany. Historians hotly dispute Bismarck's motives in this colonial drive.[2] Whatever Bismarck's final motivations, however, it is possible to see how Bismarck tied together these separate issue areas—colonial activity and Franco-German relations. Bismarck's support for France in the 1880s led to German protestations that France forget Alsace and Lorraine. Bismarck's call for a League of Neutrals (including France but excluding Great Britain) in 1884 appeared but a thinly disguised effort to draw France away from the Rhine. There is little question that Anglo-French colonial tensions provided Bismarck with an additional means to maintain a favorable balance of forces: German conflicts with Britain and German cooperation with France prevented an alignment between these two western powers.

The tentative ties between France and Germany were fragile. The French government made it clear that French colonies, no matter how high the reward in prestige, were no substitute, ultimately, for the return of Alsace and Lorraine. While the Ferry government was willing to cooperate on colonial questions, it was unwilling to endorse a more serious rapprochement with Germany without a resolution of the Alsace and Lorraine problem. Bismarck's efforts to promote an entente ended shortly after the fall of the Ferry government in 1885.

The temporary advantages derived from the interdependence of colonial and alignment-of-forces issues were threatened by yet another crisis in the Balkans. Once again, a split between Russia and Austria-Hungary confronted Bismarck with the collapse of his objectives. This crisis was initially the result of a rebellion in Eastern Roumelia—the portion of Bulgaria excised from the Bulgaria drawn up by the Russians in the Treaty of

San Stefano. At the time of the Congress of Berlin (1878), Russia demanded the retention of a large Bulgaria. The Russian government's hope was that its influence could be enhanced in the whole of the Balkans through a large and friendly "big" Bulgaria. As is so often the case in diplomatic plans, the Russian scenario did not ultimately work out. It was found that Alexander of Battenberg, the ruler of Bulgaria, was less pliable than the Tsar and his ministers had hoped. Indeed, by the mid-1880s, Russia found itself rather more content to restrict Bulgaria's size, at least as long as Alexander ruled.

The revolution of September 1885 in Eastern Roumelia, which ended in a union with Bulgaria under the rule of Prince Alexander, found Russia committed to undoing this new Balkan union. Russian demands on Turkey, who maintained nominal control over Eastern Roumelia, went unaddressed, and Russia discovered little support in either Vienna or London for its position. In November the Balkan crisis deepened with the declaration of war by Serbia on Bulgaria. Much to the surprise of the Serbians, however, Serbian forces were decisively defeated. To Serbia's dismay, Bulgarian forces, after victories at Slivnitza and Pirot, invaded Serbia. Serbian forces were only saved further embarrassment through the timely diplomatic intervention of the Austrians.

While Bulgaria and Turkey finally arrived at a mutually satisfactory agreement over Eastern Roumelia, diplomatic tensions were renewed when pro-Russian officers in Bulgaria abducted Alexander. Though Alexander finally returned to Bulgaria, the Tsar's unalterable opposition to Alexander finally led to his abdication. But Bulgarian resistance to Russian interference and pressure did not end with Alexander's abdication. A new candidate was selected to head Bulgaria, against the wishes of the Russian government. Prince Waldemar of Denmark was elected but turned it down because of threats of Russian intervention. This threat brought stern warnings from Count Kalnoky, the Austrian Foreign Minister. Bismarck had tried to resolve the conflict in part by demanding cooperation from the Bulgarians in regard to Russian demands. He was presented with a serious threat of conflict between these two crucial yet volatile allies. In fact, the likelihood of conflict between the two eastern monarchies became so serious as to warrant a Bismarckian warning to Austria-Hungary that the Dual Alliance of 1879 did not oblige Germany to support Austria in a war of aggression. While the war threat receded, the heightened tensions in the Balkans and the growing antagonism of the two eastern monarchies left the Russians totally unwilling to contemplate the possibility of the renewal of the Three Emperors' Alliance.

Thus, by 1887, due to these tensions in the Balkans, Bismarck was faced with a weakened hold over a favorable balance of forces. The early advantages of the Dual Alliance and the Three Emperors' Alliance had dissipated. The Chancellor was left with the unpleasant possibility of a discontented Russia and an isolated France seeking each other out for mutual support and protection. Bismarck took direct action, unwilling to face the defeat of his diplomatic efforts in regard to alignment of forces in Europe. On June 18, 1887, Russia and Germany signed the secret Reinsurance Treaty. While largely meaningless in regard to their mutual support against other powers, particularly France and Austria-Hungary, it provided a last formal link between Russia and Germany.

However, Bismarck did not remain content with this rather superficial alliance. Additionally, Germany supported negotiations, in 1887, among Austria-Hungary, Italy, and Great Britain aimed at blocking Russian and French influence in the Balkans and the Mediterranean. These activities culminated in a series of agreements and adherences by these three powers in two separate negotiations—the First (February 1887) and Second (December 1887) Mediterranean Agreements. The agreements provided support to Italy in case of French activity in the Mediterranean. They also provided for Austrian and British solidarity against Russian objectives in the Balkans and the Straits. Even more important than the substance of the agreements, these Mediterranean accords marked the first formal involvement of Great Britain in the balance of forces in these two decades. It is strange, given later events, that Britain's diplomatic agreement placed it, at least in the 1880s, on the same side as the Germans. For Bismarck, these interlocking agreements served as a final means to prevent France from securing a major ally from among the powers.

While Britain became embroiled in the alignment of forces issue so central to Bismarckian calculations, Britain's main concern in the diplomatic activities of the powers was focused on colonial questions. We have already noted Great Britain's conflicts with France over Egypt and quarrels with Germany in Africa and Asia. Britain's troubles with France over Egypt continued throughout the 1880s. After the debacle of the London Conference, Britain set about resolving the Egyptian issue. In 1887, five years after the initial British invasion, Britain revealed the so-called Drummond-Wolff convention, which proposed the evacuation of Egypt by Great Britain within three years, though Britain reserved the right to reoccupy Egypt in the case of disorders. However, the agreement was unsatisfactory to the French: both the French and Russians, acting in concert, forced Turkey, the nominal sovereign of Egypt, to reject the British plan. This démarche of 1887 marked a serious turn in diplomatic action for Bismarck, since it represented one of the first acts of collaboration between an increasingly isolated Russia and an already isolated France. From Britain's standpoint, it was one of a series of antagonistic actions on the part of the decades' chronic pair of antagonists— Russia and Great Britain.

In the 1870s, Russia and Great Britain had clashed head-on over the results of the Russo-Turkish War. British concern to protect the Straits from Russian control impelled Britain, more than France or Austria-Hungary, to support the shaky Ottoman Empire. Though British colonial interests were far-flung, none was more important than India. Thus, keeping the Straits open and free from Russian control was regarded as having the greatest importance by every British government.

The Balkans and Straits were not the only regions of conflict between Britain and Russia. Conflict arose in areas much closer

to India. Beginning in 1884, Russia began to penetrate territories in central Asia, moving ever closer to India. These encroachments soon extended to Afghanistan. Meanwhile, British
efforts to delimit areas of interest between themselves and the
Russians in central Asia failed. Finally, in 1886, as Russian
troops crept as far south as Penjdeh, Britain alerted reserves and
made it clear to the Russian government that further Russian
expansion risked a direct confrontation with Great Britain.
Though the Penjdeh crisis eased, British-Russian conflicts continued in the Middle East and in the Far East. These conflicts
would extend well beyond these two decades.

British colonial conflicts with the Russians served Bismarckian efforts to protect a favorable balance of states. Britain's
colonial rivalries with both France and Russia left the British
with few options but to find friends among the remaining
states—Austria-Hungary, Italy, and even Germany. As has been
discussed, a formal agreement with Austria, in 1887, secured
the status quo in the Mediterranean and North Africa against
both France and Russia. As for Anglo-German relations, earlier
colonial tensions eased considerably after 1885. Once again, the
Chancellor became supportive of British actions in Egypt; brief
informal inquiries about an Anglo-German agreement were
passed between the two governments. This easing of tension
between the two powers culminated, in 1890, in an agreement
to transfer Heligoland to Germany in return for Germany's
surrender of claims to East Africa. Even before this zenith of
cooperative diplomacy, in 1889 Germany and Britain worked
closely together to ease a serious crisis between France and
Italy.

The colonial issues thus produced for Bismarck both pluses
and minuses in the arrangement of powers. By 1887, Germany
had secured a significant number of formal arrangements in the
Mediterranean or the Balkans with Italy, Austria-Hungary and
Great Britain. Though links with Russia had been weakened
substantially with the second Balkan crisis, Russia's break with
Austria-Hungary had not irrevocably isolated Russia and Germany due to the Reinsurance Treaty. Yet already there were

disturbing signs of a growing mutual attraction between France and Russia. There was the joint diplomatic démarche against the Drummond-Wolff convention. In January 1889, a further warning of a growing rapprochement appeared with a Russian order to France's armament industry to supply the Russian army with Lebel rifles.

If French and Russian activity had become more positive, this outcome could be in part attributed to the renewal of hostilities between Germany and France. The short-lived Franco-German entente ended in 1885, soon after the fall of the procolonial Ferry government. Relations between the two countries were to remain sour for the remainder of the decade for various reasons, including border incidents as well as government changes. In April 1887, a French border official, Schnaebelé, was arrested by the Germans for allegedly carrying on espionage. Though the official was released a week later, it stirred emotions on both sides of the border.

Far more serious to the tenor of Franco-German relations was the meteoric rise of General Georges Boulanger to political power in France. Boulanger was a complex figure in Third Republic politics who was regarded as both a conservative and a republican. Of much greater concern to Bismarck was Boulanger's apparent identification, in the French public's mind, with the forces of revanche. From the Franco-Prussian War on, Bismarck had exerted what influence he had in France to maintain relatively weak republican regimes in office. The rise of Boulanger threatened, or so it appeared to Bismarck, the continuation of these weak republican administrations. Therefore, the Chancellor let it be known that Boulanger's success threatened conflict with Germany. Though appointed as a minister of war in the Freycinet government, Boulanger was dropped, subsequently, from the Rouvier administration. While Bismarck's machinations cannot be held solely responsible,[3] this temporary eclipse of Boulanger reduced the state of tensions between the two governments. The German government, for its part, assured the French that relations between the two had improved now that Boulanger no longer held office.

Besides these direct Franco-German tensions, toward the end of the 1880s there appeared a growing interdependence between Franco-German and German-Russian tensions and conflicts, and solidarity between French and Russian governments. In the spring of 1887, a Russian ukase was promulgated: it forbade foreigners to hold land along the border. Without question, enforcement of such a Russian policy was sure to have a detrimental impact on German nationals in Poland. Not without coincidence, in November 1887, the German government forbade the Reichsbank to accept Russian securities as collateral for loans.[4] As a result, by December 1888, Russian securities were placed on the Paris market. This first 500 million franc loan was just the first of many bond issues that forged close financial ties between the two countries. Both the estrangement from Austria-Hungary, Germany's long-standing ally, and the growing practical arrangements with France made a Russian-French entente increasingly attractive to both governments.

But the isolation of Russia from former allies was not completed until 1890. As long as Bismarck remained Chancellor, efforts continued to renew the Reinsurance Treaty with the Russians. Bismarck's dismissal on March 18, 1890 sealed the fate of these negotiations. The Caprivi government and the young Kaiser, William II, made it clear to the Russians that there would be no new treaty, in spite of the fact that the Russians made numerous efforts to reopen the question of renewal. Bismarck's efforts to align forces had been a continuing balancing act; the Caprivi government rejected such a strategy. It is of course true that the Austro-Russian break made it difficult to straddle the objectives and needs of both powers. With or without Bismarck, the balance of alignment was leading to the end of French isolation. But the Caprivi government's decision, particularly given the enthusiasm for some new agreement on the part of the Russians, decisively enhanced the attractiveness of new agreements between the French and Russian governments. After the failure of the Reinsurance Treaty and the renewal of the Triple Alliance, it is not surprising that what had remained a delicate suggestion of closer military cooperation between the French and Russians became a formal commitment by 1891.

The interrelationships of various issue areas and objectives over these twenty-one years reveal a bewildering complexity to the diplomatic interactions of the powers. Even a cursory glance at the historical analysis uncovers contrary patterns of inter-action. In 1873, for instance, Germany insisted France stop Catholic bishops from protesting Germany's Kulturkampf. This conflictual action resulted in a prompt French appeal to the Pope to moderate the actions of the French clergy. Yet in January 1874, a similar German warning threatening a possible German attack led, instead, to a French appeal for aid from the Russian Tsar. When Germany in 1875 threatened a possible German preventive war to forestall a strengthened French army, the French government called on the capitals of Europe for support against the Germans rather than assuaging German anger.

Anglo-Russian tensions over territory in Central Asia paral-leled conflicts at home. In the 1870s, Russia occupied the Khanate of Kiva. Such a Russian action was regarded by the British as unfriendly, yet they responded, in part, by inviting the Russian Tsar to visit Great Britain. Later, however, in the 1880s, Russian encroachments at Penjdeh resulted in British threats of war.

As a final example, we can observe the complex patterns of interactions between Germany and Italy. In 1873, Italy sug-gested a military agreement with Germany; Bismarck responded with an outright rejection of such a scheme. Later Italian schemes for German-Italian negotiations ended with Bismarck-ian comments that the road to Berlin led through Vienna. Finally, Robilant's schemes for alliance in the early 1880s found Bismarck highly receptive and encouraging. In January 1888, Germany and Italy signed a military agreement.

The diplomatic instances from these two decades demon-strate the highly varied responses to cooperative and conflictual behavior revealed by the detailed historical analysis. Looking at these isolated individual cases appears to confirm the absence of any pattern to diplomatic behavior. But rather than delve further into a small number of events, we turn instead to an examination of the entire pattern of diplomatic interactions from 1870 to 1890 between Great Britain, France, Russia, Germany, Austria-Hungary, and Italy. With this complete set of interactions, we can test systematically various explanations for the patterns of behavioral interactions, beginning with symmetry. In this way, the behavioral aapproach can extend (through the historical interactions) our general understanding of interstate behavior, without which a theory of international relations is impossible.

NOTES

1. For greater detail on the diplomatic maneuverings of France and Germany through this period, see A. Mitchell (1973) and P. B. Mitchell (1935).

2. For an orthodox diplomatic perspective, see Taylor (1938). For contemporary perspectives which focus on the domestic exigencies of the regime, see Wehler (1970) and Geiss (1976).

3. Much of the responsibility for Boulanger's dismissal can be explained by the jealousy aroused in the ranks of the other prominent political figures of the time, who distrusted Boulanger's popularity. And, indeed, Boulanger's eclipse was not permanent; for in January 1889, Boulanger was elected in the department of the Seine. Though many believed Boulanger planned to seize power after this electoral victory, Boulanger failed to fulfill the expectations of his most ardent supporters. This failure proved his undoing, and Boulanger found himself threatened with prosecution for treason. Because of this charge, he fled France for Belgium. Within two years Boulanger was dead, having committed suicide over the grave of his mistress.

4. As with most policies by Bismarck, more than one motive can be ascribed to his actions. As the great diplomatic historian W. Langer (1964: 441-442) suggests, there were several motivations simultaneously at work besides the desire to take retaliatory action against the May Ukase. These motivations included a genuine lack of faith in the Tsarist regime, a desire to undermine the position of the finance ministers, Vishnegradski, a supporter of a Franco-Russian alliance, and finally a means to discourage the military party in Russia by raising financial difficulties.

Chapter 4

THE PATTERNS OF SYMMETRY OF
THE EUROPEAN POWERS,
1870 to 1890

SYMMETRY AND THE POWERS

The key to success for either structural or behavioral models of the international system is the capacity to explain outcomes. Does the concept of symmetry provide such an explanation?

Kenneth Boulding argues forcefully for a symmetric view of interaction. Describing national perspectives, Boulding (1969: 426) asserts that "the images A and B hold of each other measured on a friendliness-hostility dimension tend to both consistency and reciprocration—if a nation A pictures itself as hostile toward B, it usually also pictures B as hostile toward it and the image is likely to be repeated in B." Furthermore, Boulding (1969: 427) argues, attitudes are likely to become symmetric over time in patterns of interaction: "If I loves J and J hates I, then either J's constant rebuff of I's affection will turn I's love to hate, or I's persistent wooing will break down J's distaste and turn it into affection."

This symmetric view is put into even a more dynamic context by Jervis (1976). Jervis details two competing models of international relations. He focuses on both the international environment—particularly the logic of the security dilemma—and the force of actor perceptions. The first model—the spiral model—parallels the symmetry of Boulding. It incorporates the strategic choices and outcomes of the Prisoner's Dilemma from game theory. This model builds consequences based on the decision makers' insecurity regarding other state actors in the anarchic world of international relations. As Jervis (1976: 65) describes it (quoting Lord Grey, the British Foreign Secretary): "The increase of armaments, that is intended in each nation to produce consciousness of strength, and sense of security, does not produce these effects. On the contrary, it produces a consciousness of the strength of other nations and a sense of fear." While each state may wish to avoid threats and conflicts, neither can afford to trust the other side. The result of this mistrust and defensive/aggressive preparation is "the argument that threats and negative sanctions, far from leading to beneficial results predicted by deterrence theory (which we will discuss next) are often self-defeating as a costly and unstable cycle is set in motion." (Jervis, 1976: 81). In this view, then, threat leads to further threats in a spiral of interaction with potentially disastrous consequences.

But this is not the only model of interaction. Indeed, much of the most recent diplomatic-strategic thinking is premised on a logic which ultimately asserts asymmetric patterns of interaction. Our strategic calculations of deterrence assume that at extreme levels of behavior, asymmetric patterns of behavior existed. Jervis (1976: 78) correctly pinpoints the key element of constrast between the spiral model and this second asymmetric model—the deterrence model—when he suggests the two models differ by providing "opposite answers to the central question of the effect of negative sanctions." The deterrence model presupposes the logic of the "Chicken Game," where mutual reward strategies dominate defect strategies in game-theory terms. Deterrence, in behaviorial terms, argues that sufficiently credible threats will result in cooperative behavior, though there may be various sequences of cooperation and threat preceding ultimate cooperative behavior from the target actor. While the most serious interstate confrontations seem to confirm this pattern, particularly since the advent of nuclear arsenals, outside the strategic arena this pattern of interaction is far less apparent. Fred Iklé (1971: 118), examining the termination of conflicts, suggests that strategic deterrence is ultimately and insufficient guarantee of cooperative responses. "A military relationship among nations based on deterrence alone may also prevent war for a long time. But if deep hostilities and the roots of sharp conflict persist, continued reliance on deterrence cannot close all avenues that might lead to war."

Indeed, numerous threats in interstate relations have resulted in increased competitive behavior, our spiral-model view. Social psychologist Morton Deutsch (1958: 277) has argued from his experimental results "that the attempt to control the other through threat of punishment is likely to be resisted, especially when the other feels that it is demeaning to allow himself to be intimidated." Yet the efficacy of cooperative behavior is not supported experimentally. In Shure et al. (1965: 116), the cooperative strategy, defined in their analysis as the pacifist strategy, apparently invited "exploitation and aggression even among those who do not begin with such intentions." At this point we have inadequate empirical evidence strategic asymmetric pattern in international relations.

These models attempt to be dynamic while remaining quite vague about the actual sequence of interaction which in this analysis is the starting point of our inquiry. Given our choice of the stimulus-response framework, we need to identify what action produces what kind of response.

Our stimulus-response framework identifies four possible patterns of interaction. On the symmetric side, there is the threat-counterthreat pattern, where conflict returns conflict, and a second pattern, what we call here the positive reinforcement

model, where cooperative actions encourage cooperative responses. This second pattern has seldom been discussed because
analysts have focused primarily on conflict and war and ignored
the wider diplomatic environment.

On the asymmetric side, there are again two patterns of
interaction. The first is where threat returns cooperation (what
we have described as the deterrence pattern). The second asymmetric pattern, logically enough, is where cooperation returns
threats. This pattern we have designated the "appeasement"
pattern. The designation is a reflection of the putative lessons of
the interwar years, during which British cooperative behavior
toward Hitler's Germany simply led to more threatening and
demanding German diplomatic behavior. The appeasement view
reinforces both the deterrence and spiral models. It assumes
that cooperative behavior in the anarchic world of international
realtions is likely to be taken as weakness. Cooperation, rather
than reinforcing cooperative responses, conveys weakness and
encourages further threats. In our analysis, this model has a
distinct independent pattern that can be tested for, unlike the
broader perspectives already discussed.

We thus have four testable patterns of interaction. If the
former patterns prevail, then behavioral interaction can be regarded as consisting of symmetric patterns. If the latter two
patterns prevail, then interstate behavior is largely asymmetric.
In order empirically to determine which patterns of interaction
prevail, we test all the interactions of the powers with the
following initial hypothesis:

Symmetry Hypothesis

*If A acts conflictually toward B, then B acts conflictually toward A;
if A acts cooperatively toward B, then B acts cooperatively toward
A.*

Of the 1433 events coded, 804 represent complete interactions—an action from one power and a response from the
target. The remaining 629 events consist of actions only—actors
receive no response from the targeted power. The no-response

TABLE 4.1   Frequency of Cooperative/Conflictual Initiated Actions

	Cooperative	Conflictual	Total
Number	576	228	804
Percentage	75	28	

actions represent an unanticipated separate category of inter-action. The size of this category represents a significant sub-group of behavior, and though we will incorporate this category where possible, the bulk of the examination will be with completed interactions.

It is interesting that the 804 events are not equally divided. As Table 4.1 indicates, there are many more cooperatively initiated actions than conflictually initiated actions. Somewhat surprisingly, these figures appear to be quite similar to ones found in another events-data analysis by McClelland and Hoggard (1969), this for the period 1966. In their analysis of a very different period of international relations, they found (McClelland and Hoggard, 1969: 715) that conflict represented 31.5 percent of all behavior; cooperation and a somewhat more neutral behavioral category—participation—represented the remaining 68.5 percent of all behavior. The findings here and in this previous study suggest that close to a 2:1 cooperation-to-conflict ratio appears commonly across system actors. These findings reinforce the view we have put forward right from the beginning of this study: too narrow a focus on crisis or conflict distorts and misrepresents the nature of international relations. As these results suggest, there is substantial cooperative behavior in interaction among states, a mixed behavior pattern that is lost when one solely focuses on crisis. Such conflict perspectives avoid describing and integrating cooperation into our understanding of the influence process.

In Table 4.2, we find the results of the Symmetry Hypothesis. These results are for the entire period and for all our

TABLE 4.2   Frequency of Symmetry of Behavior,
                     1870-1890 (Hypothesis 1)

	Total Symmetry	Symmetry of Cooperation	Symmetry of Conflict
Number of symmetric interactions	550	418	132
Percentage of symmetric interactions	68	73	58

powers. The table shows total symmetry plus symmetry broken down by categories of cooperation and conflict. The results confirm broadly our original Symmetry Hypothesis. Such a finding is indeed important, given the absence of empirical evidence for symmetry up to this point. And, just as significantly, the results reveal substantial variation between cooperation and conflict. While the Symmetry Hypothesis is supported both for cooperation and conflict, here the evidence for symmetry of cooperation is much stronger than for symmetry of conflict.

At first glance, these data, undifferentiated either by actors or time, support behaviorally, to some degree, the deterrence model. There appears to be a substantial number of instances where conflictual actions returned cooperative responses. In other words, even within the general findings of symmetry there appears to be a significant number of asymmetric conflict interactions, particularly in contrast to cooperation. The issues of deterrence in interaction are so central to the logic of diplomacy that our findings require further examination and an additional test to examine notions of "behavioral deterrence."

DETERRENCE AND THE LOGIC OF DIPLOMACY

In support of the logic of deterrence, one should find that the more extreme the conflict action, the higher the probability of a cooperative response.[1] In other words, our new hypothesis would suggest that a more serious action, verbal or physical, would be taken as more credible and would more likely result in target compliance, at least given the logic of the deterrence model.[2] This speculation on deterrence leads us to make and test a second hypothesis on behavioral interaction.

Behavioral Deterrence Hypothesis

The more extreme the conflictual stimuli, the less probable a symmetric response.

In order to test this second hypothesis, the conflictual actions were partitioned into two different groups. All conflictual actions scaled above 42 (that is, 42 to 50) on the "Corkeley" scale were defined as warnings—less extreme actions—whereas those actions below 42 (42 to 0) were defined as extreme conflict actions.[3]

Table 4.3 provides us with a breakdown of the two patterns of interaction—the symmetric one (threat-counterthreat) and the asymmetric pattern (deterrence). The Deterrence Hypothesis would lead us to speculate that for all our dyads, in the cases of deterrence, the greater percentage would be extreme actions—stimuli below 42. Of the total of 96 cases where threat leads to cooperation, 49 cases, or 51 percent of the cases, are initiated by substantial threat. However, of the 132 cases where threat leads to a threatening response (threat-counterthreat), 82 cases, or 62 percent of the actions, consist of substantial threats leading to conflictual responses. Indeed, if we take the total number of extreme initiations (131), then 63 percent result in conflictual responses; only 37 percent of the more conflictual extreme initiatives result in cooperative responses. Thus, although at a first glance the Behavioral Deterrence Hypothesis seems supported by the patterns of symmetric interaction for conflict, a closer inspection fails to support this hypothesis. Our findings do not pretend to test strategic deterrence and certainly not the contemporary stress on nuclear credibility and commitments. Nevertheless, the behavioral deterrence perspective examines notions of deterrence in the broader diplomatic

TABLE 4.3 Behavioral Deterrence Hypothesis

			Conflict-Cooperation			Conflict-Conflict			
Actor	*Target*	*N*	*Extreme Actions*	*Warnings*	*Percentage of Extreme Actions*	*N*	*Extreme Actions*	*Warning*	*Percentage of Extreme Actions*
Germany	All Targets	28	19	9	67.9	29	19	10	65.5
Britain	All Targets	19	11	8	57.9	30	17	13	56.7
Russia	All Targets	20	9	11	45.0	32	19	13	59.4
Austria	All Targets	14	1	13	7.1	12	3	9	25.0
France	All Targets	10	7	3	70.0	17	15	2	88.2
Italy	All Targets	5	2	3	40.0	12	9	3	75.0
Totals		96	49	47		132	82	50	

environment. There is no question that elements of strategic thinking have become a commonplace in thinking about the influence process. What the failure of the Behavioral Deterrence hypothesis suggests is that notions of the "hard" or "firm line" in bargaining, largely acquired from strategic notions, are not supported in the wider patterns of interaction examined here. Such findings are crucial as we credit diplomacy outcomes in the international system.

VARIATIONS IN DYADIC SYMMETRY

Having examined some of the variations in symmetry of cooperation and conflict, let us further sketch those differences by dyads. In Table 4.4, each country is taken as the actor, and the symmetry levels are displayed for all its targets (the remaining five powers). The lower half of the table repeats the breakdown, but in this portion of the table the actor becomes the target for the remaining powers. Table 4.4 points out the range of symmetry levels within the categories of conflict and cooperation, depending on the particular actor initiating behavior or acting as a target. Both cooperation and conflict vary substantially. Cooperation levels range from Italy's low of 57.8 percent to France's high of 76.8 percent. Italy receives conflict for cooperation initiated more frequently than any other power. France, on the other hand, receives cooperation back for cooperation initiated more than any power during these twenty-one years. For conflict, the range runs from Austria-Hungary's low of 46.2 percent all the way to Italy's high of 70.6 percent. You'll note further that only two actors have symmetry levels of conflict that either contradict or nearly contradict the Symmetry Hypothesis. These two are Germany and Austria-Hungary. Italy, on the other hand, more than any other country, receives conflict for conflict initiated.

Table 4.4, therefore, reveals the evident range of symmetry even at this partly disaggregated level. If the Symmetry Hypothesis is supported—strongly for cooperation, less so for conflict—the challenge presented by these findings is to be able to

TABLE 4.4 Symmetry Levels: Actor to All Targets and Targets to All Actors

Actor	Total Symmetry		Symmetry of Cooperation		Symmetry of Conflict	
	Number	Percentage	Number	Percentage	Number	Percentage
Germany-Targets	(194)*	68.6	(137)	75.9	(57)	50.9
Britain-Targets	(169)	66.9	(120)	69.2	(49)	61.2
Russian-Targets	(155)	71.0	(103)	75.2	(52)	61.5
Austria-Targets	(122)	69.7	(96)	76.0	(26)	46.2
France-Targets	(83)	72.3	(56)	76.8	(27)	63.0
Italy-Targets	(81)	60.5	(54)	57.8	(17)	70.6
Targets-Germany	(228)	67.5	(163)	71.8	(65)	56.9
Targets-Britain	(143)	69.9	(104)	74.0	(39)	59.0
Targets-Russia	(136)	66.2	(90)	72.2	(46)	54.3
Targets-Austria	(148)	65.5	(118)	68.6	(30)	53.3
Targets-France	(86)	74.4	(54)	77.8	(32)	68.8
Targets-Italy	(63)	71.4	(47)	76.6	(16)	56.3

*Number of interactions.

extend our explanation of the logic of diplomacy to encompass an explanation of the patterns of symmetry across the various pairs of Great Powers. As we have already argued, structural explanations appear to provide the most likely source of explanation. At least superficially, power differences indeed appear to explain some of variations identified in Table 4.4. Italy, for instance, was the weakest of our Great Powers at this time. If power explains differences in the symmetry of behavior, then Italy's weak power might explain why Italy, more than other powers, receives conflict for conflict initiated. Also, its weak power position may account for the frequent conflictual responses to Italy's cooperative initiatives.

Austria-Hungary's low symmetry of conflict may be explained by another important international relations structural concept—status. Led by Prince Metternich, Austria-Hungary was regarded, early in the nineteenth century, as the premier diplomatic power. Metternich was largely responsible for the creation and maintenance of the Congress System which shaped international politics for a large portion of the nineteenth century. Even at the time of our investigation (with Austria-Hungary's defeat at the hands of the Prussians and troubled domestic politics), Austria-Hungary was still regarded as a Great Power. The low symmetry of conflict may be accounted for by this status position. A relatively high status may have encouraged frequent cooperative responses for conflict actions initiated.

The descriptions provided so far are rather ad hoc explanations. However, in the next chapter we shall attempt to explain the variations in symmetry employing key structural variables—power, status, and alliance.

RESPONSES AND NO RESPONSES

Before plunging into explanations for the variations of symmetry, some attention, while still at this general level of analysis, should be paid to no responses. As we pointed out, "no response" reactions to initiation of interactions form a substantial portion of our events—in fact, almost 44 percent. We find that of all initiations, where no immediate response was evident, 60 percent are cooperative and 40 percent are conflictual, a figure somewhat higher for conflict than was our response category.

When looking at symmetry for "no responses" we cannot employ the same definitions used previously. There is little in the literature of international relations about no-response initiatives: Studies of interaction presuppose stimuli and responses. Since we have classified no immediate-response initiations according to conflict or cooperation categories, it seems appropriate to suggest variations for these differences of cooperation or conflict. Without greater explanation (this is taken up in the next chapter), we might suggest that the relationship between no immediate response and cooperation and conflict is:

No-Response Hypothesis

The ratio of no response to total actions is higher for cooperative actions than for conflictual actions.

Our assumption underlying this hypothesis centers on the idea that cooperative actions are more frequent and therefore more likely to be ignored. We assume here that ignoring conflict is more likely to lead to costly outcomes; ignoring cooperation is not likely to be as damaging to the target state. As a result, for our pairs of states, the ratios of cooperative no responses to all cooperative responses should be higher than ratios of conflictual no responses to all conflictual initiatives.

Table 4.5 displays all the no responses and total responses and their ratios for all the powers. In summarizing this table, we find that the majority of cases do not bear out the No-Response Hypothesis. Of the twenty-eight directed dyads where we calculated a ratio for both cooperation and conflict, only 25 percent of the cases confirmed our hypothesis. In fact, looking at all the dyads the ratio of cooperative "no responses" to total cooperative initiatives comes to .40; the ratio for conflict comes to .52. The results, contrary to expectations, reveal that, conflicts, not cooperation, is more likely to be ignored. Only one actor,

TABLE 4.5 The No-Response Hypothesis

Actor	Target	No. of Responses		No. of Responses		Total No. of Initiations		Ratio of Coop.	Ratio of Conf.
		Coop.	Conf.	Coop.	Conf.	Coop.	Conf.		
Germany	All Targets	37	57	155	60	292	117	.53	.51
Britain	All Targets	129	49	73	76	93	125	.58	.61
Russia	All Targets	103	52	48	51	151	103	.32	.50
Austria	All Targets	96	26	38	19	134	45	.28	.42
France	All Targets	56	27	31	32	87	59	.36	.54
Italy	All Targets	64	17	33	13	97	30	.34	.43

Germany, supports the hypothesis. Such a finding might suggest that in international politics, while it might be costly to ignore a conflictual signal, response to a threat might be even more costly. The findings of Table 4.5 may reveal a mechanism for interstate tension reduction. Ignoring conflictual stimuli may be a diplomatic means employed by target states to diffuse conflictual actions that might otherwise lead to greater and more dangerous conflict interactions.

While the no immediate responses involve a relatively substantial frequency of all initiations by our powers under investigation, the lack of literature on no responses makes further analysis difficult. When possible, we shall reintroduce questions involving no immediate response, but in general we will devote our energies to uncovering the explanation for the variations in levels of symmetry for completed stimulus-response patterns. Those efforts begin immediately with the next chapter.

NOTES

1. In a more social psychological setting, Kaplowitz (1973: 535-572) tested various theories of deterrence. One of the initial assumptions set out for testing by Kaplowitz suggested: "the greater the credibility of the threat source, the more compliant the target (subject)." Leng (1980), in a more international setting, also argued and tested similar notions of behavioral deterrence. But, as Kaplowitz demonstrated, the rationalistic approach was not confirmed strongly in his experiments. Such a finding lends support to the evidence found here using interstate behavior.

2. This statement is not an absolute statement. At some point—at the far extreme—the severity of the punishment is so great that defiance may be the only possible response. Within our parameters of behavioral deterrence, this statement should stand as it is stated in the Behavioral Deterrence Hypothesis.

3. Any division like this is artificial in some sense. This particular division was first employed in an earlier paper entitled "Statecraft in the Analysis of International Relations: Reward and Punishment in the Bismarckian System 1870-90," presented at Peace Science Society (International) Northeast, Carleton University, Ottawa, April 5-6, 1978. This categorization was chosen, in part, because the physical versus verbal distinctions between categories become clear around 42 on this scale.

Chapter 5

STRUCTURES AND THE LOGIC OF DIPLOMACY

DEFINING A LINK BETWEEN
SYMMETRY AND POWER

The Symmetry Hypothesis (Chapter Four) has generally proved correct for the entire twenty-one years and all the dyads. But Chapter Four also revealed that there were significant variations in cooperative and conflictual symmetry among the powers and over time.

An immediate questionable assumption of the analysis in Chapter Four is that all actors and all targets are identical in all aspects but their interactions. This assumption of equality among the European powers is highly restrictive and historically unrealistic. While many characteristics differentiate states, none is more frequently discussed in international relations than power. The realist approach to international relations puts power at the center of international politics. The classic theory of international politics—"the balance of power"—is largely about power differences, and power's impact on international relations outcomes. National capabilities remain a key structural variable in quantitative international relations (Singer 1972; Bremer, 1980; Ferris, 1973). Frequently power is seen to be to international relations what money is to economics—the basic unit of measurement and explanation.

Any attempt to link power and influence requires answers to two key questions: first, what is the link between power as an attribute and interaction? Second, how do we define power as an attribute? From there we can then examine whether the variations in symmetry between countries are explicable through differences in power—the structural variable. Certainly, given the focus on power by both the traditional and quantitative literature, we would expect power as a key structural variable, to explain the difference in the patterns of interaction among the powers.

THE POWER HYPOTHESIS

The literature on power or influence does not provide a strong guide to the relationship of power to interaction. What is available derives mainly from social psychology (Blau, 1964; Chadwick-Jones, 1976; Homans, 1951, 1961; Thibaut and Kelley, 1959). Social psychology finds the influence process central in the examination of the behavior of individuals and groups. In work on trust and threats, Deutsch (1958, 1973) appears to argue that dependency may determine the probability of particular responses. Pruitt (1965: 401) seems to confirm this view when he argues:

The first set of hypotheses concerns dependence and interdependence. It seems reasonable to suppose that one party is more likely to under-react to provocations from the other party, the more dependent it feels itself to be on the other party's good will.

According to Pruitt, dependency seems to produce less than an identical (symmetric) conflictual response.

The concept of attribute power can certainly measure dependencies. Often, power dependence is defined as the disparity between what one state holds of a particular form of power and what another state holds. For example, in a two-power world where state A holds all the power, defined here as guns, and where the other, state B, possesses no power, no guns, state B would appear to be at the mercy of, or dependent upon A. If A demands B join it in alliance or suffer the consequences, B will be unlikely to respond in a threatening manner. In our two decades, having defeated the French armies on the battlefield and the French people at Paris, Germany demanded France accept its terms of peace. The French, with little military power remaining and little will to employ it, felt compelled, in 1871, to cooperate with Germany and accede to its harsh demands.

But if dependency helps us to utilize attribute power in an analysis of behavioral interaction, the literature remains unclear on how dependency explains symmetry of behavior. It seems possible to argue that dependent relations between actors might lead to forms of asymmetric responses, as in the previous examples, or quite the reverse, that dependencies are more likely to lead to symmetric responses.

The nature of cost, however, might help us identify the relationship of attribute power and symmetry in a dyadic setting. We mentioned in Chapter Four the concept of cost in regard to response/no-response interactions. We suggested that cooperative stimuli might be less costly for a state to ignore than conflictual actions. Cost may help us here to link symmetry of behavior and attribute power. Robert Dahl (1957), in his exegesis of power in politics, failed to include the concept of costs. His classic definition went: "A has power over B to the extent that he can get B to do something B would not otherwise do" (Dahl, 1957: 202-203). John Harsanyi (1962), in a critique of Dahl's works, pointed out this exclusion of the "cost" concept in Dahl's explanation of the influence process. As Harsanyi argued, "a realistic quantitative description of A's power over B must include, as an essential dimension of this power relation, the costs to A of attempting to influence B" (Harsanyi, 1962: 70).[1]

Thus, taking both cost and power together, states which are more equal in power (the analysis will define this shortly) would be more likely to respond in like manner to behavioral interactions, whether cooperative and conflictual. The relative equality of power in a dyad should result in the relative equality of costs of behavior to both states, increasing the likelihood of symmetric patterns of interaction for a dyad. Where the power held within a dyad is unequally divided (one state possessing a much larger share than the other), we hypothesize that greater asymmetries of behavior will be the outcome. The greater the inequalities in power, the more likely the differences in the cost of the influence process. These cost inequalities should result in threats inducing a greater frequency of cooperation and cooperation, eliciting conflict more frequently.[2] With this perspective in mind, the following hypothesis represents the presumed relationship of behavioral interaction and power as an attribute.

Hypothesis (Power Hypothesis)

The more equal the power between A and B, the higher the percentage of symmetric interactions; the more unequal the power between A and B, the lower the percentage of symmetric interaction.

DEFINING POWER

The Power Hypothesis links symmetry of interaction to our structural variable—attribute power. We still have to define what constitutes attribute power. Much has been written on the dimensions of power in international relations.[3] While the exact dimensions vary from analysis to analysis (Choucri and North, 1975; Ferris, 1973; Rosecrance et al., 1974; Rummel, 1971; Singer et al., 1972), there emerges almost common agreement on the various dimensions on national power. Capabilities in international relations seem to include a military dimension which includes the means to directly coerce adversaries, a resource dimension capable of being mobilized in times of crisis or need by a nation, and an economic dimension defining the wealth, technology, and industrial strength of the country.[4]

We have taken these common dimensions as our starting point, but within those broad categories—the military dimension, the mobilization and resource dimension, and the industrialization dimension—we have tried to identify power attributes that were important to the statesmen of the period. Power definitions change. Pig-iron production may be a crucial power indicator in 1850; in 1920 it is steel. The total horse population may be a crucial indicator of reserve power for a state in the nineteenth century; after 1930, it is not horses but tanks. In an analysis such as this, with the emphasis on context and the historical character of international politics, we focus on indicators largely recognized by the decisionmakers themselves. While superficially less "scientific" in one sense, this approach relates to the purpose of this particular analysis— remaining close to the historical reality of the period 1870 to 1890. As a result, we have collected yearly data for all countries on the following dimensions.[5]

Military Power Dimension
   military personnel
   military expenditures
   number of ironclads

Mobilization and Resource Power Dimension
   railroad density
   population
   total revenues
   revenue per capita

Industrialization Dimension
   railroad mileage
   coal output
   iron output
   steel output
   trade value (exports plus imports)

Both because the attributes which constitute power remain unclear and because the degrees to which attributes influence actor interaction[6] remain in dispute, we shall test the Power Hypothesis in as broad and differentiated a manner as possible.

The analysis will test each indicator separately (summary table for results, Table 5.1). Then the analysis shall combine various similar power indicators together and test these. Finally, all the indicators will be combined into one index—The Combined Power Index—and tested with differences in symmetry. In this way, we hope to examine fully the differences of power and the relationship of attribute power to the differences in symmetry of interaction—the logic of diplomacy.

COUNTRY PROFILES— INDEXES OF POWER

The following is an attempt to summarize the power relations of the Great Powers of this period through the various indexes we have constructed. You will note that we have combined two of our dimensions of power—mobilization, and resource and industrialization. It was necessary to do so because both proportional measures—railroad density and revenues per capita—were excluded from the index building: we could not determine percentage shares for these two variables. Nevertheless, we have three indexes to compare and contrast power relations among the states—the military index (three variables), the mobilization and industrial index (seven variables), and the combined power index (ten variables). (For an actual comparison of the percentage shares see Appendix B.)

GREAT BRITAIN

From viewing the three indexes—military, industrial, and combined power indexes—it is hard not to regard Britain as the premier power in Europe through these twenty-one years. The inclusion of seven industiral or mobilization indicators emphasizes Britain's strengths. Not surprisingly, Britain dominates both the mobilization and industrial index and the combined power index. The reasons are evident. Britain is first in pig iron, crude steel, coal, and trade value by very large percentages. In the industrial dimension it ranks lower than first only on railroad mileage, where it is second to Germany in the 1870s, and then drops as low as fourth by the 1880s. With resources and mobilization, it ranks first on railroad density and either second or third on government revenues and revenues per capita. Only with population does Great Britain rank relatively low, fifth in this case.

Britain's power is less dominant on the military index. It is ranked third behind Russia and France. Though Britain holds a premier position in ironclads, it is ranked last for its share of military personnel and only third or second with military expenditures, always behind France and at times behind Russia in the mid 1870s.

While Britain's position is dominant on the combined power index, as we noted earlier, this is a transitional period of power. Analyzing the industrial sectors, Ashworth (1966: 34) has described Britain's changing position in the following way:

> British industry did not stagnate; it more than doubled its output between 1870-1913. But in the world as a whole there was a fourfold increase, and whereas Britain in 1870 produced nearly one-third of the world's output of manufacturing in the closing years of the 19th century it produced only one-fifth, and in 1913 about one-seventh.

Even the British navy, the heart of Britain's military capability, suffered a decline in this period. Only the threat of a combined Russian-French challenge in the Mediterranean, late in the eighties, and the later German challenge, spurred the British to reverse the decline in their naval strength. While Great Britain remained Europe's largest power, new powers had already appeared. It would not be long before these new powers would be ready to challenge Britain's dominance.

FRANCE

Unlike Britain, the zenith of French glory and power obviously had passed by the 1870s. The defeat at the hands of the Prussians was a cruel blow to a proud nation. France's military loss revealed some glaring weaknesses: it adoption of modern instruments of power, particularly rail and logistical planning, had not worked well. Yet the French reaction to defeat was to increase military expenditures and to create new, larger armies. Indeed, on the military index France sustains a second position to Britain on ironclads, a second position to Russia on personnel (though Germany remains close) and is itself first on military expenditures through most of the period. As a result, through much of these years France ranks first or second on the combined military index. Despite these military efforts, by the end of the 1880s France's position is only a little ahead of third-place Britain.

The mobilization and industrial power index reveals, however, France's true weakness—its industrial development. While Kemp (1971: 249-253) points to industrial concerns such as Schneider-Creusot as examples of French industrial leaders in Europe, the overall performance of France's economy was slow, particularly in comparison to Germany. Even with trade, where France is second to Great Britain, it loses its second position to Germany by the mid 1880s.

France's mobilization and resources follow the same pattern. France possesses the third-ranked share of railroad density behind Britain and Germany and a second position on population that becomes fourth by the 1870s, behind Russia, Germany, and Austria-Hungary. Only with revenues and revenues per capita do the French hold the dominant position.

France's position on the combined power index sums up its declining power position. France ranks an overall second to Great Britain at the beginning of the decade. By 1878 to 1880, its percentage share of power is equal only to Germany's, both tied behind Great Britain. For the remainder of the period, however, Germany's share increases while France's share declines.

GERMANY

Germany represents the last of the three "Great Powers," compared on the combined power index. For Germany, this twenty-one-year period presages the rapid growth in German power that would make Great Britain Germany's only European rival by the end of the century.

These are years of rapid change for the newly created German Empire. While ranked third overall in power, by the end of the first decade Germany surpasses France, its chief rival. A quick glance at the industrial, and the mobilization and resources power dimensions reveals Germany's powerful and growing position. Germany is first in railroad mileage and second only to Britain in pig iron, steel, and coal. Though Britain retains the dominant shares, Germany's are increasing for almost every one of these indicators. Germany's trade rank, which is third behind both Britain and France, becomes second in the mid 1880s. For the mobilization indicators, Germany holds second position with railroad density, population, and revenues (it becomes first on revenues by the end of the 1880's). Finally, with revenues per capita it moves from a third or fourth position behind Britain, France, and Austria to a position second only to France.

Somewhat surprisingly, it is Germany's military indicators which seem to restrain its overall power ranking.[7] At the start of the 1870s, Germany ranks last of the powers in ironclass. As early as the mid 1870s, its position has increased to fourth, but it remains there through the rest of the period, behind Britain, France, and Russia. Even on military expenditures Germany ranks fourth initially. It is only in the last time period that Germany achieves a dominant position on this indicator. Germany's military personnel indicator maintains a third rank behind Russia and France for the entire twenty-one years. But even if these military indicators limit Germany's share of combined military power, by the end of the 1880s Germany military share has doubled and is only slightly lower than Great Britain's. This factor, combined with Germany's industrial growth, leaves Germany second in combined power by the end of the 1880s.

RUSSIA

By most accounts, these twenty-one years all but exclude the period of rapid Russian industrialization that begins only in the mid-1880s.[8] For Russia industrialization required solving the problem of capital. It was not until the administrations of Burge, Vyshenegradsky, and Witte that it was possible for Russia to stabilize its currency, thereby encouraging sustained foreign investment.

The industrialization index places Russia fourth. This likely inflates Russia's position, since the analysis uses railroad mileage and population and not railroad or population density. As it is, Russia places first on the population index (it is indeed ranked lower on population density). As for railroad mileage, it is only fourth, ranking ahead of Austria and Italy. Other industrial and mobilization indicators more clearly suggest Russia's limited power position. On railroad density and revenue per capita, Russia ranks last of all the powers; on revenue, pig iron, coal, and trade, Russia ranks fifth ahead of Italy only. Only on steel does Russia reach a higher position, ranking fourth ahead of both Italy and Austria by the 1880s.

The combined power index places Russia in a solid fourth position ahead of both Austria-Hungary and Italy. Russia's military power explains this. On the military index, Russia ranks first in percentage share by the early 1870s and maintains this position almost continuously thereafter. Though ranked third behind Britain and France on ironclads, it is first in personnel. On military expenditures it is second to France early in the 1870's, first during the Russo-Turkish War, dropping finally to fourth by the end of the 1880s behind France, Britain, and Germany. It is evident from these last figures on military power that although Russia continued to lag behind in industrial might, the Russians remained committed to maintaining military power. This commitment explains the fourth-place ranking on the combined power index.

AUSTRIA-HUNGARY

Austria-Hungary and Italy vie with each other for the smallest shares of all three indexes. Of all the indexes, Austria-Hungary ranks last only in the case of the military power, and this only from the mid-1880s on. For military power Austria ranks last on ironclads and fifth on military expenditures. Only on personnel does Austria's rank substantially vary, ranking fourth, ahead of both Britain and Italy.

Overall, Austria-Hungary suffered from an inefficient government and limited resources, exacerbated by the politics of ethnic conflict. Moreover, Austria's geography, which is rugged, made railway construction difficult and expensive. Coal was not abundant, and Austrian industry was forced to rely frequently on water power, which also limited its industrial growth. As a result, Austria-Hungary ranks fifth on the industrialization and mobilization index and fifth on the combined power index. With the individual industrial measures, Austria-Hungary ranks fifth or sixth on railroad density, revenue per capita, railroad mileage, steel and trade. For the remainder, revenues, pig iron, and coal, Austria-Hungary ranks fourth ahead of Russia and Italy and fourth on population ahead of Britain and Italy. Austria-Hungary, in comparison to other powers such as Great Britain, Germany, and France, can hardly be called a Great Power at all.

ITALY

Italy presents a picture similar to Austria-Hungary's. Its resource base is poor; its transportation system is even worse than Austria-Hungary's; industrialization in all but a few areas remains nonexistent. Sustained growth for Italy does not come until after a prolonged depression in the building and banking sectors of the Italian economy which does not end till 1896. As a result, Italy ranks last on both the industrial index and the combined power index.

On the individual attributes, Italy ranks lowest in population, revenue, railroad mileage, pig iron, crude steel, and coal. The exceptions to this pattern occur with revenue per capita where Italy ranks fifth and trade value, where she ranks fourth or fifth. By the end of the 1870s, Italy holds the lowest share of this indicator as well. On railroad density alone does Italy maintain a consistent fourth ahead of both Russia and Austria-Hungary.

Italy breaks with the pattern of lowest power only on the military index and here only in the late 1880s. On ironclads it is fifth ahead of Austria. It is last on expenditures, and last on personnel, though by the mid-1880s Italy does rank above Britain. Even with the somewhat higher standing on the military index, the general picture presented here, without question, is that of the smallest power in this constellation of six Great Powers.

TESTING THE POWER HYPOTHESIS

Having briefly indicated our indicators and the relative standing of our powers, we can proceed to test the relationship between attribute power and influence—the symmetry of behavioral interaction. In order to compare the relationship of power to symmetry of interaction, the analysis calculated the dyadic rank of power differences for all our definitions of power and the rank of symmetry for every dyad every three years (see Appendix A for the logic of an ordinal time series analysis). The dyads were then ranked and the two ranks compared. Every dyad was compared with every other dyad in each three-year period. For the paired comparisons, more 70 percent in the same direction was regarded as significant while less than 30 percent in the same direction was regarded as significant as well. (see Table 5.2 for an example of a complete paired-comparison test). The required level of significant comparisons to either confirm the hypothesis or confirm the opposite of the hypothesis was 50 percent.

Table 5.1 summarizes the findings (all individual power tests and all index tests) between power differences and symmetry of behavior—the Power Hypothesis. From the table it is clear that not one of the definitions of power either confirms the Power Hypothesis or confirms the opposite of the Power Hypothesis for this entire period.

A closer look at the combined power index (Table 5.2) may provide some insight into our negative findings. The table displays the paired comparisons of all the time periods. For the

TABLE 5.1   Summary of Paired-Comparison Tests of the
Power Hypothesis

	Percentage of Time Periods that confirm the Power Hypothesis				Percentage of Time Periods that confirm the opposite of the Power Hypothesis			
	Symmetry of Cooperation		Symmetry Conflict		Symmetry of Cooperation		Symmetry of Conflict	
Military Expenditure	2/17*	12%**	1/17	6%	4/17	24%	6/17	35%
Military Personnel	0/17	0	0/17	0	2/17	12	5/17	29
Number of Ironclads	0/17	0	1/17	0	0/17	0	5/17	29
Military Power Index (3 variables)	1/17	6	1/17	6	2/17	12	7/17	41
Population	0/17	0	2/17	12	3/17	18	1/17	6
Railroad Density	0/17	0	3/17	18	3/17	18	0/17	0
Total Revenues	0/17	0	2/17	12	1/17	6	4/17	24
Coal Output	1/17	6	1/17	6	3/17	18	2/17	12
Pig Iron	1/17	6	2/17	12	4/17	24	2/17	12
Crude Steel	0/17	0	2/17	12	4/17	24	1/17	6
Railroad Mileage	0/17	0	0/17	0	1/17	6	3/17	18
Trade Value	1/16	6	0/11	0	3/16	19	4/11	36
Revenues/Capital	0/17	0	2/17	12	6/17	35	6/17	35
Industrial Index (7 variables)	1/17	6	1/17	6	3/17	18	2/17	12
Combined Power Index (10 variables)	1/17	6	2/16	12	3/17	18	2/17	12

*   above 70% is regarded as a significant paired comparison; below 30% is regarded as a significant
     paired comparison.
**   50 percent of time periods regarded as a significant finding.

hypothesis to be confirmed, we should find that the closer the
relative shares of power are between any two states, the greater
the degree of symmetry of behavior there should be for the
dyad. Since we are employing an ordered metric and not just a
simple ranking (see methodology appendix), we may find the
shares of power are so divided that there are actually larger
differences between the top ranked states than between the
bottom ranked states. In these instances, we should find the
highest dyadic symmetry between those states ranked as low
powers since they are actually more equal in power shares. On
the other hand, if the power shares are relatively equal among
the top ranked powers, then it should be these powers who

TABLE 5.2   Paired Comparisons: Combined Power Index

	Symmetry of Cooperation		Symmetry of Conflict	
1870-73*	24		43	
1873-75	33		70	
1874-76	51		60	
1875-77	67		60	
1876-78	58		57	
1877-79	82		71	
1878-80	66		52	
1879-81	69		61	
1880-82	58		50	
1881-83	54		36	
1882-84	53		10	
1883-85	67		27	
1886-88	24		47	
1887-89	22		33	
1888-90	46		29	
Percentage of time periods that confirm the Power Hypothesis	1/17	6%	2/16	12%
Percentage of time periods that confirm the opposite of the Power Hypothesis	3/17	18%	2/17	12%

*The first period includes an extra-year due to lack of interactions.

**Above 70 percent is regarded as significant; below 30 percent is regarded as significant.

should exhibit the higher symmetries of behavioral interaction.[9]

In the combined power index we find that the greatest disparities exist between Britain, the first-ranked power, and the remaining powers. Throughout the two decades, dyads with Great Britain represent ones with the most disparate shares of power. Initially, Austria-Hungary and Italy, the two lowest-ranked powers on the combined power index, have the most equal shares of power. But as early as the 1873-1875 period, the Germany/France dyad possesses the most equal shares of power. Indeed, through most of the two decades, dyads including combinations of Russia, France, and Germany maintain relatively equal power shares. These dyads should also exhibit the higher symmetries of behavior. But symmetry does not seem to be ranked in relation to our combined power index in the order required to confirm the Power Hypothesis.

Looking at a number of dyads[10] ranked by the combined power index highlights the failure to relate our broadest measure of power and actor interaction (see Table 5.3 for all individual comparisons). For example, Germany/Austria-Hungary, when compared over time, does reveal a strong confirmation of the Power Hypothesis with symmetry of cooperation. This is not repeated for conflict symmetry.

When we turn to our second and third most powerful states, France and Germany, we are looking at the most consistently equal power dyad of our two decades. Comparing this particular dyad with several others reveals several individual confirmations but no consistent pattern. With France/Germany and Germany/ Italy, the high symmetries of behavior for France/Germany result in a relatively high confirmation of the Power Hypothesis with both conflict and cooperation. A Germany/Austria-Hungary, Germany/France comparison confirms the hypothesis with the symmetry of conflict; however, it fails to do so with the symmetry of cooperation. When Germany/Austria-Hungary is compared with Germany/Russia, a more equal power dyad, though one ranked lower than Germany/France, the results are even less confirmatory. Yet Germany/Russia compares well with high/high equal power dyad Germany/France. Here Ger-

TABLE 5.3 Individual Dyad Comparisons of the Power Hypothesis (Combined Power Index–10 Variables)

Ger/Brt	*Ger/Rus*		*Ger/Frn*		*Ger/Aus*		*Ger/Itl*		*Brn/Aus*		*Brn/Frn*		*Brn/Aus*		*Brn/Itl*		*Rus/Frn*		*Rus/Aus*		*Rus/Itl*		*Frn/Aus*		*Frn/Itl*		*Aus/Itl*	
	56	44	73	100	60	36	30	38	0	25	25	50	64	100	57	25	14	0	75	69	-	-	100	0	50	67	36	25
Ger/Brt	16	16	15	11	15	11	10	8	11	12	12	8	11	3	7	4	7	8	12	13	-	-	3	1	4	3	11	8
			93	83	40	50	50	44	25	17	47	0	70	100	43	100	75	50	43	36	-	-	0		75	0	73	22
	Ger/Rus		15	12	15	12	10	9	12	12	15	9	10	3	7	4	8	8	14	14	-	-	3	1	4	4	11	9
					43	88	75	83	42	89	46	60	82	100	50	100	71	100	69	64	-	-	0	-	67	0	70	33
			Ger/Frn		14	8	8	6	12	9	13	5	11	3	6	2	7	7	13	11	-	-	3	-	3	2	10	6
							100	38	50	0	62	50	100	100	100	0	0	0	31	73	-	-	0	-	50	0	0	33
					Ger/Aus		9	8	10	8	13	8	11	3	6	3	6	3	13	11	-	-	2	-	4	4	10	9
									0	25	25	43	14	100	25	0	25	0	100	86	-	-	-	-	100	100	50	29
							Ger/Itl		4	4	8	7	7	3	4	1	4	4	7	7	-	-	-	-	3	3	10	7
											20	20	100	100	100	100	0	0	9	20	-	-	100	0	0	100	0	20
									Brt/Rus		10	5	8	2	6	3	6	6	10	10	-	-	3	1	1	1	7	5
													56	100	50	100	0	0	58	50	-	-	67	-	50	100	27	0
											Brt/Frn		9	3	6	1	3	3	12	6	-	-	3	-	4	2	11	7
															50	-	50	0	80	100	-	-	100	-	67	-	38	100
													Brt/Aus		6	-	6	2	10	3	-	-	3	-	3	-	8	3
																	40	0	100	100	-	-	100	0	0	100	40	100
															Brt/Itl		5	2	4	3	-	-	2	1	1	1	5	1
																			20	0	-	-	0	-	-	-	71	0
																	Rus/Frn		5	6	-	-	2	-	-	-	7	3
																					-	-	0	100	75	0	33	13
																			Rus/Aus		-	-	3	1	4	3	9	8
																							-	-			-	-
																					Rus/Itl		-	-			-	-
																									100	0	50	100
																							Frn/Aus		1	1	2	1
																											0	25
																									Frn/Itl		3	4
																											Aus/Itl	

Abbreviations: Ger=Germany; Brt=Britain; Frn-France; Aus=Austria-Hungary; Itl=Italy; Rus=Russia.

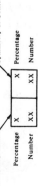

Symmetry of Cooperation — Symmetry of Conflict

Percentage	X	X	Percentage
Number	XX	XX	Number

many/France, which is ranked higher with less disparate shares of power, exhibits generally higher symmetries of cooperation and conflict, as the Power Hypothesis would suggest. Thus, it appears that the dyad Germany/Austria-Hungary has a symmetry of cooperation level too high for the confirmation of the Power Hypothesis.

Historically, there are evident reasons for this. Austria-Hungary's eagerness to sign the Dual Alliance late in the 1870s encouraged cooperative responses from Austria-Hungary to Bismarck's early inquiries; later, in the 1880s, Austria-Hungary eagerly supported many of the German Chancellor's actions to solve the second Balkan Crisis, particularly Bismarck's suggestions to seek negotiations with Great Britain and Italy. The Balkan turmoil is responsible, moreover, for a level of symmetry of conflict which results in poor comparisons with relatively equal power dyad Germany/Russia. The symmetry tables reveal that Germany/Austria-Hungary's high symmetry of conflict was due largely to Austria's conflictual behavior, which elicited conflictual responses by Germany. In response to Austria's threats against Russia, Germany was forced to warn Austria-Hungary that it, Germany, would not support Austria-Hungary in its designs against the Russians.[11]

Germany/Austria-Hungary is not the only case to reveal the difficulties of confirming our hypothesis. Germany/Italy's symmetry of conflict and cooperation reveals a strong confirmation of the Power Hypothesis: Germany/Italy's symmetries of conflict and cooperation are consistently lower than France/Germany's. When we turn to Germany/Russia we find the results, particularly for conflict, disconfirming. Germany/Italy maintains a symmetry-of-conflict level higher Germany/Russia's, particularly in the early 1880s. Though Germany/Italy's symmetry of conflict is ranked somewhere about the average, Germany/Russia's ranks very low for an equal power dyad. In this case, both Germany and Russia turn aside mutual warnings rather than returning conflict following the signing of the Three Emperors' Alliance. Yet when we compare Germany/Italy with Britain/Germany (remembering Germany/Italy

should have the higher symmetry), we find that Germany/
Italy's symmetry of conflict is not high enough. Finally, when
we compare Germany/Italy with Germany/Austria-Hungary
(Germany/Austria-Hungary is more equal in power shares than
Germany/Italy), it appears too high again.

These individual cases only emphasize the general findings of
power and symmetry revealed in the general paired comparisons. We find ourselves unable to confirm the Power Hypothesis
or the opposite of the Power Hypothesis. Differences in power
seem incapable of explaining variations in the levels of symmetric interaction. Power, however, while a vitally important structural variable, is not the only attribute defining the international system. In the next section we continue our efforts to
build in a structural explanation with our interaction approach
by focusing on status and status inconsistency.

DEFINING A LINK BETWEEN
SYMMETRY AND STATUS

Though status or prestige was a concept known and used by
diplomatic historians, its most serious examination in international relations has emerged relatively recently. Social
psychology and sociology have richly developed concepts such
as status, rank, and status inequality. In quantitative international relations the most focused work has proceeded within
the Dimensionability of Nations Project, under the direction of
Rudolph Rummel. As was noted earlier, the early foundations
of this project built on field theory (Lewin, 1951). Later
versions examined social field theory and finally status field
theory.

The status literature provided international relations analysts
(East, 1972; Galtung, 1966a, 1966b, 1971; Rummel, 1971;
Wallace, 1971) with some very specific identifications of the
relationship of status to behavior. From the sociology literature,
the international system was described as being stratified, and as
East (1972: 99) points out, "the stratification of states has
important consequences for that state's behavior in a wide range
of activities."

THE STATUS HYPOTHESES

One of the difficulties in the literature on status in international relations is defining exactly what it is. The sociological literature derives status from concepts of inequality and indeed has identified two specific forms—achieved and ascribed status. Particularly in notions of inequality these distinctions in status are vitally important. Achieved status is generally defined by those indicators which indicate a state's capacity for development, indicators that can be manipulated by the direct actions of the states. Ascribed status, on the other hand, denotes factors the nation has less control over, or as Wallace (1971: 26) has suggested, those factors "which [are] fixed by the structure and culture of the system and thus not alterable by the actor's own efforts." As a result of these distinctions, achieved status is generally defined in capability or power terms. In our analysis, we can employ our indicators of capability, particularly the Combined Power Index, as the measure of achieved status.

Ascribed status has proven more controversial to define and measure. Ascribed status is generally seen as containing dimensions of wealth and prestige. There has been some disagreement on this point. The DON project, while recognizing the prestige dimension, has nonetheless excluded it[12] from its measurement of ascription in international relations. Yet prestige is an evident concept in international politics. Today countries such as Sweden, India, and Switzerland today hold valued positions in the international system; wealth alone does not define their status. Equally, in our period, Austria-Hungary and Italy retain Great Power status today but not solely as a result of power or wealth. Thus, following the lead of Brams (1969), East (1972) Midlarsky (1969), Rosecrance et al. (1974), and Wallace (1971), I will include prestige in the desinition of status. In fact, we will use two indicators of prestige—diplomatic recognitions and diplomatic representations. The first measures how the international system regards the six powers. The second represents an intra-European comparison because it measures the number of diplomats and consuls that each Great Power stations in each other's territories, including colonies. These two measures are combined to provide a measure of ascribed status as completely as possible.

Unlike power, the contemporary focus on status provides a valuable set of propositions which can be useful in relation status and rank (the summed total of status measures) to interaction. Status is most frequently measured categorically. In status nomenclature, high status is designated "T" for Topdog while low status is referred to by "U" for Underdog. Given the two definitions of status we find that four distinct actor types are possible: TT for high status across both dimensions, UU for low status across both dimensions, and then those countries that are mixed UT or TU.

The basic axiom of status is that called the "Axiom of Upward Mobility." As Galtung (1966b: 158) described this axiom, "All individuals seek maximum total rank and the only stationary status set is one with only high statuses." The search for high status has direct outcomes on patterns of actor inter- action. Since high status is desired, there is a tendency for high-status actors (TT) to interact more with one another than with low- or mixed-status actors. As a result, "individual inter- actions increase as a positive function of rank" (Rummel, 1975: 164). Thus, high-status actors will act most cooperatively with other high-status actors; low- or mixed-status actors will direct their actions to high-status actors, though interactions will not be as cooperative. These arguments on interaction and behavior are generalized across all status types by Galtung's proposition: "The higher the total rank of a pair or (n-tuple), the more interaction there will be between the units in the pair or (n-tuple), and the more associative the interaction" (1966a: 142). Status field theory provides a similar hypothesis called the "Cooperation Theorem." In both cases it is suggested that the higher the joint rank of a pair of actors, the more cooperative the behavior between these two actors. Thus, we can see a means to link status and behavioral interaction. For our pur- poses, associative (cooperative) behavior in symmetry terms can be defined as *both* a high symmetry of cooperation and a low symmetry of conflict. These definitions provide the last link necessary for the following hypothesis between status and our concern, symmetry of behavioral interaction.

Hypothesis (Cooperation Hypothesis)

The higher the joint status of dyad A and B, the higher the symmetry of cooperation and the lower the symmetry of conflict.

The Cooperation Hypothesis represents just a part of the extensive concerns of status and status field theories. Indeed, the major focus of status theory in international relations is directed far more to status inconsistency—the inequality of status dimensions within and between actors—and the effects of status inequality on behavior. Status inconsistency, or inequality, is a key status concept, linking stratification to behavior. At the extreme, it is argued (Midlarsky, 1969; Wallace, 1971), status inconsistency may lead to international warfare. Status inconsistency leads to aggressive or dissociative behavior (Galtung, 1966a, 1966b). This suggests a further hypothesis linking status inconsistency directly to our behavioral measure—symmetry of behavior.

Hypothesis (Status Inconsistency)

The greater the status inconsistency of dyad A and B, the higher the symmetry of conflict and the lower the symmetry of cooperation.[13]

Given the various types of status, this hypothesis requires some further adumbration. Because we rank and compare dyads, we find there are actually two forms of inconsistency. There is the inconsistency of status within the status dimensions of an actor and the status inconsistency between the actors (within and between the dyads). Looking at the inconsistencies of status across the dimensions of a single actor, a state may have high achieved status but have low ascription, or the state may have high ascription and low achieved status. One way of regarding status inconsistency is simply to examine the *magnitude* of incongruence. It follows that dyadic analyses would total the individual magnitudes and order all the dyads by the total of absolute differences in status (Wallace, 1971).

An alternative is to be more specific about the kinds of inconsistency. Galtung has argued (1966a: 142) that states seek to avoid incongruence, but "if efforts to obtain rank-equilibrium (status inconsistency) are frustrated, aggression will result." Therefore, agrression is not just a result of the existence of status inconsistency. In addition, achieved status is greater than ascribed status or ascribed status greater than achieved status. According again to Galtung (1966a: 142), of the two types of inconsistency, aggression is more externally oriented when the inconsistency is achieved status greater than ascribed status as opposed to instances of ascribed greater than achieved. In order to take these differences into account, the initial rankings of magnitude will be reordered, not only according to the magnitude of the pairs, but also according to the *types* of inconsistency.

There is, finally, one additional degree of complexity of status inconsistency, based on the nature of the dyadic actors. Galtung (1966a, 1966b) takes into account in his analysis not only the magnitude and the type of inconsistency, but the consistency of status ranks for the individual *actor* and, as an extension, the *pair of actors* in interactions. As a result, Galtung provides us with a set of axioms ordering the various combinations of actors according to their degree of associative or cooperative behavior. There are, for our four status types (TT, UU, TU, UT), three axioms of topdog-underdog status which determine the outcomes of interaction (Galtung, 1966b: 164). The first axiom suggests that the lower the number of links, the less associative the relations. In a TT-TT interaction, there are two links (the number of same status rankings between actors), whereas there is but one in a TT-TU interaction. The second axiom asserts that the lower the number of topdog links, the less associative the relations. Theoretically, then, a TT-TT relationship should be more associative with its numerous topdog links than a dyad of UU-UU. Finally, if no links exist, e.g., TT-UU, ordering can be established from the third axiom, which argues that the lower the total rank distance (the total differences in total rankings comparing joint status dimensions), the less associative the relations. Therefore, in our TT-UU case the distance is maximal, while in TU-UT there is no rank distance.

In our analysis, with four actor types, there are ten possible dyadic combinations. By employing these three axioms, all ten combinations can be ranked according to their hypothesized degree of cooperative behavior (Galtung, 1966b: 164):

1. TT-TT
2. TU-TU, U1-UT
3. UU-UU
4. TT-TU, TT-UT
5. TU-UU, UT-UU
6. TT-UU
7. TU-UT

With this ranking, we have a third and final means to test our Status Inconsistency Hypothesis, including all three elements in our status ranking—magnitude of inconsistency, type of inconsistency, and type of dyad interaction or actor inconsistency. When testing the Status Inconsistency Hypothesis we produced from the most simple to the most complex, with each test adding a degree of further complexity to the status inconsistency definition.

When we look at the status rankings for the Cooperation Hypothesis, Great Britain dominates all the major status categories. Though Britain's share of status rank (achieved plus ascribed) declines steadily over the two decades, she remainś the unrivaled status power. Germany and France hold significantly smaller shares of status than Great Britain. Germany displays a slow but marked increase in overall status, though it is clear that this is largely a result of achieved status. France, on the other hand, suffers a decline in its overall status during the two decades, this largely a result of an achieved status decline. Indeed, by the three-year period 1884-1886, Germany's status rank surpasses that of France. Germany and France are followed by Russia, Austria-Hungary, and Italy, in that order. Both Austria-Hungary and Italy maintain relatively stable status percentage shares; Russia's share grows steadily, a result of increases in both status dimensions.

The picture varies when we look at status inconsistency as opposed to total status rank. When comparing the rankings of the countries we need to point out the magnitude of the differences in status shares, the types of differences, and the categories of actor status, whether topdog or underdog. In order to establish actor type, each instance of status for all actors is compared to the systemic average. Where the status share is below that average, then an underdog or U is designated; where it is above the mean, a topdog or T is inserted.

In the twenty-one years examined, we find that in any one three-year period the maximum number of different actors is three out of a possible four. Where this occurs, we find the number of different dyad types equals five.[14] However, the most frequent pattern, for our analysis, includes only two types of actors—TT, UU—providing only three unique dyadic combinations: TT-TT, TT-UU, UU-UU. A brief review, by country, will help sort out the various status-inconsistency patterns of the powers from 1870 to 1890.

COUNTRY PROFILES—
STATUS INCONSISTENCY

GREAT BRITAIN

While Great Britain is the highest status-ranked power, it also appears to be, along with Italy, the most status-inconsistent power. Even though these two are the most inconsistent, the inconsistencies appear in opposite directions. For Great Britain, the status inconsistency is determined by a relatively larger achieved status than an ascribed one. The inconsistency declines over time and we find, by 1878-1880, that Italy achieves distinction as the most status-inconsistent power. While Britain's inconsistency declines, it nonetheless sustains a TT status throughout the twenty-one years.

FRANCE

While France ranks as the next-highest status power, closely followed by Germany, we find that both exhibit the smallest status inconsistencies between achievement and ascription. It is interesting that France's inconsistency declines through most of the 1870s. Beginning in the 1880s, it begins to increase again. In the change from decreasing inconsistency to increasing inconsistency, France shifts from greater achievement than ascription to greater ascription than achievement. Thus, while France begins the 1870s as a TT actor, its decline in achieved status is large enough, by 1886, to alter France's definition to a TU actor—an actor with topdog ascribed status but underdog achieved status. Even though the definition changes, France still ends the decade as the least status-inconsistent actor of all our powers.

GERMANY

Germany maintains a high-status position throughout our period and one substantially higher at the end of the 1880s, than at the beginning of the 1870s. Like France, Germany is a largely status-consistent power, at least in the first twelve years. Its small inconsistencies are a product of greater achievement than ascription. What is noticeable by the middle of the 1880s, however, is the escalation in the achievement share, which boosts Germany's inconsistency ranking. Except for the first time period, Germany maintains a consistent TT ranking throughout.

RUSSIA

Russia, ranking in the middle of our status rankings, exhibits a substantial inconsistency created by greater achievement than ascription. The inconsistency remains fairly constant, though through the early 1880s there is a slow increase which fails to abate until the mid-1880s. The maintenance of the same status inconsistency share is reflected in its actor type as well; throughout the twenty-one years Russia displays a UU status pattern.

AUSTRIA-HUNGARY

Austria's pattern is relatively similar to Russia's. It is ranked right next to Russia toward the bottom end of the status ladder. Its inconsistency share is also about the same magnitude as Russia's. We find Austria-Hungary's inconsistency is exactly opposite to Russia's. Austria-Hungary's inconsistency results from too much ascription; Austria-Hungary's poor power position influences her overall type of status inconsistency. However, this variation in inconsistency does not affect the type of status actor Austria-Hungary is; like Russia, it maintains UU rankings throughout the two decades.

ITALY

Except for the first time period, Italy holds the smallest share of status of all our powers. However, this does not determine status inconsistency. We find that, along with Great Britain, Italy maintains the most status-inconsistent shares of all. By 1880 and continuing till the end of the decade, Italy is the most status inconsistent. Unlike Britain its inconsistency is a product of far greater ascription than achievement: it is a status power without much power. Like Russia and Austria-Hungary, through both decades Italy maintains a UU actor status type.

With this brief overview, plus our indicators and hypotheses defined, we are ready to test how well dyadic rankings of status explain variations in the level of symmetry (Cooperation Hypothesis). In addition, we can examine the relationship between status inconsistency—defined in several ways—and symmetry (Status-Inconsistency Hypothesis).

TESTING THE STATUS HYPOTHESIS

Table 5.4 summarizes the various forms of ordinal time-series paired-comparison tests of the Cooperation and Status Inconsistency Hypotheses. As the table dramatically reveals, none of the tests of either hypothesis shows a significant relationship be-

TABLE 5.4   Summary of Paired Comparisons for Cooperation and Status Inconsistency Hypothesis

	Percentage of Time Periods that Confirm the Cooperation Hypothesis				Percentage of Time Periods that Confirm the Opposite of the Cooperation Hypothesis			
	Symmetry of Cooperation		Symmetry of Conflict		Symmetry of Cooperation		Symmetry of Conflict	
Achieved Status	0/17*	0%**	2/17	12%	0/17	0%	0/17	0%
Ascribed Status	0/17	0	1/17	6	1/17	6	0/17	0
Status Rank (achieved plus Ascribed Status)	0/17	0	1/17	6	0/17	0	0/17	0

	Percentage of Time Periods that Confirm the Status Inconsistency Hypothesis				Percentage of Time Periods that Confirm the Opposite of the Status Inconsistency Hypothesis			
	Symmetry of Cooperation		Symmetry of Conflict		Symmetry of Cooperation		Symmetry of Conflict	
Status Inconsistency:								
Magnitude	5/17	29%	1/17	6%	1/17	6%	3/17	18%
Type	1/17	6	1/17	6	1/17	6%	4/17	24
Actor	1/17	6	1/17	6	1/17	6	6/17	35

* above 70% is regarded as a significant paired comparison;
  below 30% is regarded as a significant paired comparison.

** 50% of time periods is regarded as a significant finding.

tween our structural variable—status—and symmetry of interaction.

Like our various tests of power, our tests of the Cooperation Hypothesis provided a wide variation in the dyadic rankings. In order to test the hypothesis, we totaled the separate shares of the fifteen pairs of dyads rather than calculating the differences, as with power. Most rankings then proceeded from dyads of combinations of large status holders to combinations of small ones. However, there were occasions where the differences between large and small status holders were great enough so that mid-ranked combinations ended up higher on the metric ordering. Even so, the results were not significant.

Looking a little closer at the final test of status inconsistency (a test that includes differences in magnitude, type, and actor) we can see why status seemed unable to help explain the variations in the patterns of interaction (see Table 5.5 for all individual dyad comparisons). Initially in our data we have two topdogs—France and Britain. Germany establishes itself as a topdog by 1873 and maintains its topdog status from that point on. As a result, these three dyads—Britain/Germany, Britain/ France, and France/Germany—are ranked at the top of status table. They should exhibit the highest levels of associative behavior—high symmetry of cooperation and low symmetry of conflict. But individual dyad comparisons with less associative dyads—Russia/Austria-Hungary, Italy/Austria-Hungary, for instance—reveal mixed patterns of confirmation of the hypothesis. While a comparison of Britain/Germany with Italy/Austria-Hungary shows a relatively high confirmation of the hypothesis on cooperation, it shows a confirmation of the opposite of the Status-Inconsistency Hypothesis for conflict. The picture is made more complex by the fact that France lost its topdog status in 1886. It is therefore characterized as a TU status country, lowering the rank of a dyad with France in it. Comparisons of dyads with France in them show widely varying findings. There appears to be no consistency of comparison with the symmetry of cooperation. If there is any consistency at all, it is in the direction of confirming the opposite of the hypothesis for the symmetry of conflict. The patterns of individual comparison don't improve when we compare dyads which are consistent underdogs, such as Russia/Austria-Hungary, with inconsistent and less associative dyads, such as Russia/Germany or Austria-Hungary/Germany.

These individual findings only reinforce the broader general comparisons. The findings still leave us unable to integrate structural explanations with the logic of diplomacy.

However, we turn to a final structural variable—alliance. Partly because of alliance's unique characteristics, it is the structural variable which is most likely to forge a link between structure and diplomacy.

TABLE 5.5 Individual Dyad Comparisons of Status-Inconsistency Hypothesis (Magnitude, Type, Actor)

Each cell is shown as two pairs of numbers — Symmetry of Cooperation (Percentage / Number) and Symmetry of Conflict (Percentage / Number) — given here as `coop% conf% / coop# conf#`.

	Ger/Rus	Ger/Frn	Ger/Aus	Ger/Itl	Brt/Rus	Brt/Frn	Brt/Aus	Brt/Itl	Rus/Frn	Rus/Aus	Rus/Itl	Frn/Aus	Frn/Itl	Aus/Itl
Ger/Brt	38 44 / 16 16	86 27 / 14 11	7 50 / 15 12	50 25 / 10 8	0 25 / 11 12	21 88 / 14 8	64 0 / 11 3	57 25 / 7 4	71 0 / 7 8	23 62 / 13 13	·	0 · / 3 1	25 75 / 4 ·	64 25 / 11 8
Ger/Rus		67 0 / 15 12	53 50 / 15 12	50 8 / 10 8	25 75 / 42 13	40 0 / 15 9	33 100 / 9 3	57 100 / 7 4	57 100 / 7 0	57 29 / 14 14	·	100 100 / 3 ·	0 4 / 4 ·	58 44 / 12 9
Ger/Frn			43 8 / 14 8	50 54 / 10 12	42 12 / 12 13	54 20 / 13 5	82 3 / 11 0	50 4 / 6 2	71 0 / 50 100	77 10 / 13 10	·	3 ·	67 0 / 3 2	90 17 / 10 6
Ger/Aus				75 17 / 10 6	45 100 / 11 8	31 50 / 13 8	100 0 / 11 3	100 33 / 6 3	6 3 / 5 4	23 27 / 3 11	·	3 ·	75 50 / 4 4	0 56 / 10 71
Ger/Itl					0 75 / 5 4	75 38 / 20 80	71 100 / 9 8	25 0 / 4 3	40 75 / 6 6	100 0 / 9 7	·	67 100 / 3 ·	100 100 / 3 3	50 6 / 10 7
Brt/Rus						10 5	0 100 / 8 2	5 100 / 50 0	71 0 / 7 4	11 70 / 33 10	·	3 ·	0 · / 1 ·	0 80 / 7 5
Brt/Frn							56 3 / 9	60 1 / 5 ·	17 0 / 6 3	12 7 / 89 3	·	100 100 / 3 ·	25 100 / 4 2	45 33 / 11 6
Brt/Aus								5 ·	6 3 / 5 1	9 0 / 100 0	·	100 0 / 2 1	67 0 / 3 1	38 0 / 8 3
Brt/Itl									20 0 / 5 1	100 0 / 80 0	·	100 · / 2 ·	0 1	0 3 / 4 0
Rus/Frn										80 0 / 5 6	·	100 0 / 3 1	100 · / 1 ·	71 3 / 7 3
Rus/Aus											·	·	75 25 / 4 4	33 89 / 9 9
Rus/Itl												·	·	0 0 / 1 1
Frn/Aus													·	0 75 / 3 4
Frn/Itl														100 100 / 1 1
Aus/Itl														

Abbreviations: GER = Germany, BRT = Britain, RUS = Russia, AUS = Austria-Hungary, FRN = France, ITL = Italy.

Symmetry of Cooperation — Percentage / Number · Symmetry of Conflict — Percentage / Number

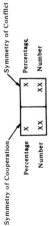

Symmetry of Cooperation	Symmetry of Conflict
Percentage	Percentage
Number	Number

103

THE ALLIANCE HYPOTHESIS

One of the evident difficulties of employing structural variables is the relative conceptual distance these variables appear to have from the logic of diplomacy. Alliance, our third structural variable, is, on the other hand, a more directly political attribute than either of the other structural variables. Prima facie, it appears to be a variable more directly sensitive to behavior than either previous attribute. Like power, it is intimately bound up with the balance of power (Butterfield and Wight, 1966; Gulick, 1955; Hinsley, 1963; Organski, 1958). Furthermore, in the contemporary quantitative literature much work has been focused on alliance, both in testing the balance of power (Singer and Small, 1966) and in testing the concept of alliances more generally (Friedman et al., 1970; Holsti et al., 1973; Rosecrance et al., 1974; Wallace, 1973). All this research points up how important alliances are in explaining international relations outcomes. For all the reasons just mentioned, alliances seem to offer the best possibility of explaining variations in symmetric interactions.

Before testing this relationship it is necessary to link theoretically alliance and symmetry. Partly because the great bulk of research on alliances has been focused on explaining the outcomes of crisis, the onset of war, and war termination, we must find a logic which defines the relationship of interaction—the broad patterns of diplomacy—to alliance. Once again, the literature on relational power seems to provide a suitable means for specifying the Alliance Hypothesis.

As with power, we can use concepts of dependence and cost with alliance to formulate a suitable proposition between alliance and symmetry of behavior.

Alliances by their very nature entail mutual dependencies. They define obligations of mutual support or protection. Alliances may provide economic assistance or military aid. They may announce expressions of friendship. But the formal nature of alliances promotes some manner of commitment. Therefore, we can suggest that the greater the number of alliances between two actors, the greater the dependence between the two actors. Alternately, the absence of alliance or commitment indicates mutual independence of obligation (and the absence of trust). Therefore, just as with power, more alliance and less alliance commitment between actor A and actor B describes the degree of mutual dependence or independence. Following the former argument on power, one would argue that the greater the dependence (more alliance), the greater the costs of identical behavioral patterns. The greater the independence—that is, the fewer the alliance commitments between states—the more equal the costs of behavioral interaction. With these relationships in mind, the hypothesis for alliance and symmetry suggests:

Hypothesis (Alliance Hypothesis)

The less allied A and B are with each other, the higher the percentage of symmetric interactions; the more allied A and B are with each other, the lower the percentage of symmetric interactions.

DEFINING ALLIANCES

In this test of alliances we are only concerned with formal "legal" mutual commitments; but there are several types of formal commitments. Singer and Small (1966: 1) have suggested three distinct alliance forms: defense pacts, which oblige some form of military intervention; neutrality or nonaggression pacts, which avoid participation in conflict by some signatories; and entente alliances, which are commitments where partners agree to "cooperate in a crisis." Thus, like power, alliance is defined in several distinct ways. The distinctions are significant enough that we want to take account of those differences when we measure dependence. In particular, we want to include in the analysis the generally accepted view that defense commitments are a more significant category than the other two (Russett, 1974). As a result, while including all formal alliance commitments between and among our powers, the analysis gives greater weight to defense pacts than either neutrality or entente commitments.[15]

In order to calculate the degree of alignment/independence between the fifteen dyads, all the alliances for these twenty-one years[16] were identified (see Table 5.6). For each alliance, the signatories to the treaty, the inception and termination dates of the agreements, and, where possible, the powers which acceded or adhered to the alliance were gathered. From this latter information we then calculated the total number of months of adherence to a particular alliance for various dyads (see Appendix B). In this scheme the total number of agreements between actor A and B times the number of alliance-months each participates represents the degree of dependence of these two states.[17] From these figures we can then establish the ranks of alliance-months for our dyads over the twenty-one years (see Appendix B).

As can be seen from Table 5.6 the number of formal alliances of all types is surprisingly high for such a limited period. There are, in fact, ten alliances of one kind or another. All our powers except France participate in at least one alliance, the majority in far more than that. These twenty-one years, then, provide a period where we are able to differentiate alliance commitments among a relatively large number of pairs of states.

TESTING ALLIANCES AND SYMMETRY

What the list of alliances (Table 5.6) cannot adequately reveal is the importance of one statesmen—Prince Otto von Bismarck—in the creation of each one of these commitments. Few statesmen have had as much written about them as has Chancellor Bismarck.[18] The assessments run from the sublime to the almost derogatory. Today, after all this research, there exists no single definitive assessment of the man and his diplomatic career.

While there is no consensus on Bismarck's motivations or his qualities as a stateman, all perspectives identify the centrality of this German Chancellor in the international politics of the period. As we have noted, the period 1870-1890 was marked by numerous alliances with Germany, Bismarck at the center of all these agreements. The first series of agreements involved both Germany and Russia, and Russia and Austria-Hungary. The

TABLE 5.6   Alliances from 1870 to 1890

Name	Signatory States (Includes Adherences)	Inception Date	Termination Date	Classification
Three Emperors' League	Austria-Hungary Germany Russia	06/1873	06/1878	Military and Entente
Budapest Convention	Austria-Hungary Russia	01/1877	06/1878	Neutrality
Dual Alliance	Austria-Hungary Germany	10/1879	1914	Defense
Three Emperors' Alliance	Germany Russia Austria-Hungary	06/1881	06/1887	Neutrality
Triple Alliance	Germany Austria-Hungary Italy	05/1882	1914	Defense
Romanian	Austria-Hungary Germany (Romania)	10/1883	1914	Defense
	Italy	05/1888		
Reinsurance	Germany Russia	06/1887	1890	Neutrality
First Mediterranean Agreement	Great Britain Italy	02/1887	1890s?	Entente
	Austria-Hungary Spain Germany	05/1887		
Second Mediterranean Agreement	Great Britain Austria-Hungary Italy	12/1887	1890s?	Entente
	Germany Italy	01/1888	1914	Defense

German-Russian pact was military in nature; the Russian-Austrian was not. Together they collectively became known as the Three Emperors' League. For Germany, the Three Emperors' League provided support against France. In addition, according to Bismarck, it was designed to provide monarchical solidarity against a new order based on a social republican principle (Bismarck, 1966: 251). The Three Emperors' League thus linked the three eastern monarchies. We should find in testing our hypothesis that these three dyads, Germany/Russia, Germany/Austria-Hungary, and Russia/Austria-Hungary, should be related to low symmetries of both conflict and cooperation throughout the 1870s, commencing in 1873.

Monarchial solidarity was a difficult condition to maintain, as Bismarck was to find out. As early as 1875, Bismarck found himself at loggerheads with Russia over threats made by Germany against France. Bismarck's assertion placed the onus for the strains with the Russians. The tensions in the Three Emperors' League "were caused in 1875 by the provocations of Prince Gortchakov, who spread the lie that we intended to fall upon France before she had recovered from her wounds" (Bismarck, 1966: 252).

But tensions over France with his erstwhile allies were not the sole difficulty; much as Bismarck had foreseen, the real obstacle in the path of a continuing Three Emperors' League was Russian/Austro-Hungarian rivalry in the Balkans. Efforts to impose reforms on the Ottoman Empire by the European powers created just such frictions. In the short run, competing objectives could be resolved, but the long-term prognosis was more difficult. In fact, early European efforts to settle the Balkan nationalities question resulted in a series of two Russian/ Austrian agreements which were ostensibly arranged to settle outstanding conflicts of interest. More darkly, the Budapest Convention defined Austrian interests in the Balkans in an effort to secure Austrian neutrality and leave Russia a free hand there. With Austrian neutrality guaranteed, Russia then proceeded to declare war on Turkey.

But, as was pointed out earlier (Chapter Three), if Russia won the war, it lost the peace. British threats of war, and Austrian anger at what it saw as unequal Russian gains against Turkey, culminated in a European call to review Russia's settlement with Turkey. The resulting Berlin Congress saw Russian gains in Bulgaria reduced and Austrian claims to Bosnia and Herzegovina guaranteed. While these results angered Russia, it was Bismarck's attitudes at the Congress which had the most immediate impact on European politics following Berlin. "At the Congress, Bismarck often supported the Russians, but on the large issues he stood by Great Britain and Austria" (Schmitt, 1934:4).

The Russians, particularly Foreign Minister Gorchakov, displayed public anger at Bismarck's actions, but Russian protests and notes provided Bismarck with the ammunition he needed to persuade a reluctant William I to agree to a treaty with Russia's Balkan rival, Austria-Hungary. This agreement, signed in October 1879, pledged both parties to aid each other if either was attacked by Russia. The Dual Alliance's intent seemed to protect Austria-Hungary from Russian attack. However, Austria was unwilling to commit the same support for defense against France in the treaty.

The Dual Alliance remained a cornerstone of German-Austrian policy until 1918, though the motives for its signing remain unclear. For our immediate interests, however, the Dual Alliance enables us to further distinguish degrees of dependence between the various country dyads. For the time comparison, 1877-1879 (see Appendix B), the Budapest Convention leaves Russia/Austria ranked highest on alliance, followed by Germany/Austria—a result of both the Three Emperors' League and the Dual Alliance—followed in turn by Germany/Russia. In the 1880s, however, as a result of the Dual Alliance, Germany/Austria established itself as the dominant dependent dyad. It remained the most allied dyad through most of the remainder of the decade. If we are to establish confirmation of our Alliance Hypothesis, all these dyads should be related to relatively low symmetry levels in contrast to the remaining dyads.

The Dual Alliance marked a dramatic change in diplomatic tactics; it concretely revealed to the Russians their isolation from former League compatriots. According to Waller (1974: 215), the Russians had decided to seek an arrangement with Berlin before the Austro-German negotiations had actually begun; the news of these negotiations made them more determined to reach an understanding. In 1881, the three monarchs once again concluded an alliance—this to replace the Three Emperors' League. Most of the clauses of the agreement clarified the various interests held by the parties in the Balkans, particularly for Russia and Austria. In addition, all three governments in this Three Emperors' Alliance pledged that if one of the contracting powers found itself at war with a fourth, the other two would remain neutral.

The alliance network was complicated further by two additional agreements. The first was the long-sought Triple Alliance of Germany, Austria, Hungary, and Italy. Signed in May 1882, the agreement largely secured Italian neutrality in case of an Austro-Russian war. Furthermore, the agreement promised German support if Italy were attacked by France and Italian support for Germany from a Russian attack. Austria-Hungary, which had never strongly supported an arrangement with Italy, participated by agreeing not to form engagements of any sort against the other two parties. The Triple Alliance was important largely because it ended Italian isolation from the other powers and strengthened its position against its chief rival, France. Furthermore, according to Schmitt (1934: 17), it was hoped this alliance would "strengthen the position of the Italian government against the Papacy."

This spate of treaties ended with the second of our two complicating alliances, signed in secret by Romania, Germany, and Austria-Hungary in late 1883. Suggested first by Bismarck as a league of peace to Austrian Foreign Minister Kalnoky, this idea was enthusiastically pursued by Kalnoky in the form of an agreement with Romania. Romanian antipathy toward Russia paved the way to an early agreement. This signing further strengthened Austria's position in the Balkans. The agreement provided that Romania would fight if Austrian territory adjacent to it was invaded by Russia. More importantly, Germany adhered to this treaty at its signing, further linking Austrian and German policies. Thus, by 1883, Germany/Austria, by far, was the most allied dyad, followed by Germany/Italy and Austria/Italy. Of those allied, Germany/Russia and Russia/Austria were the least allied of the dyads. Confirmation of our Alliance Hypothesis will be strengthened by lower symmetry ranks for Germany/Austria, Germany/Italy, and Austria/Italy both against the remaining allied dyads and against dyads totally independent of alliances, such as Britain/France, Russia/France, and others.

Crisis in the Balkans in the mid-1880s brought additional changes to the alliance network. Acute tensions arose from the rebellion in Bulgaria which culminated in Bulgaria and Eastern Roumelia being joined together under the authority of Prince Alexander of Battenberg. Though Russia had sought a "big" Bulgaria in 1878 (Treaty of San Stefano), by the mid-1880s Bulgarian willfullness had convinced Russia to maintain a limited Bulgaria. The rebellion, in September 1885, and the proclamation of a large Bulgaria brought immediate protests by Russia. To complicate the picture further, Serbia, a strong ally of Austria-Hungary, declared war on Bulgaria for compensation. Serbia's defeats at the hands of the Bulgarians led to direct Austrian interference in the Bulgarian situation, threatening further Russia's position.

Bismarck, eager to avoid the deepening rift between the two Balkan rivals, urged on both his partners his long-standing plans to demarcate spheres of interest in the Balkans. Unable to gain either Austrian or Russian acceptance of such a plan, and unable to find sufficient common ground to extend the Three Emperors' Alliance, Bismarck offered the Russian government the possibility of a solely Russian-German agreement to avoid Russia's complete isolation. After much bargaining between Bismarck and Shuvalov, an agreement was signed. This pact, the Reinsurance Treaty, guaranteed Russia's neutrality in a German conflict with France as long as Germany did not attack France, and Germany's neutrality in a Russian conflict with Austria-Hungary as long as Russia did not attack Austria-Hungary first. Furthermore, clauses provided German support for Russian claims in Bulgaria and the Straits. For all the clauses, the agreement was limited. It only delayed, but did not prevent, Russia's breach with Germany.

Bismarck, unwilling to leave the Balkan situation in such a volatile state, acted at the time of the Reinsurance negotiations to strengthen the Triple Alliance and to block possible Russian advances in the Balkans by urging further agreements among powers such as Austria-Hungary, Italy, and Britain. In early 1887, the Triple Alliance was renewed. Additional clauses were added to bring Italy closer to both Austria-Hungary and Germany. At almost the same time, Italy and Britain discussed the possibility of an agreement to guarantee the status quo in the Mediterranean. England, though wary of Italian ambitions and adamant in refusal to support Italy in a war against France, finally agreed in February 1887 to a treaty of mutual support in the Mediterranean against any differences arising between Britain, Italy, and a third power. Meanwhile, Bismarck had been concerned enough about the outcome of Italian-British negotiations to take the unusual step earlier of calling on the British ambassador and urging on him the necessity of some agreement with Italy. This British-Italian agreement (the First Mediterranean Agreement) was extended further by the adherence of Austria-Hungary to the agreement, in March, and Spain's adherence in May 1887. In turn, Germany and Austria adhered to the Italian-Spanish exchange of notes.

Even with all these exchanges of notes, the agreements in the Mediterranean continued. Toward the end of 1887, negotiations between Austria-Hungary Italy, and England began. In December 1887 they resulted in a Second Mediterranean Agreement. This second agreement, besides affirming the status quo in the Mediterranean, committed all three powers to prevent pressure being exerted on Turkey from external sources from Russia. Germany, remained officially uncommitted to the agreement, though heartily supporting measures arranged between all three powers.

The final commitment in this spate of agreements came early in 1888, with the signing of a military convention between Germany and Italy. The agreement drew Italy ever closer to the Central Powers—Austria-Hungary and Germany—by providing for an Italian attack on France in case of a Russian-French attack on Germany and Austria-Hungary.

With this 1888 agreement, the complicated network of alliances signed while Bismarck was Chancellor finally came to an end. Fittingly, Bismarck's departure, in 1890, was followed by the first dismemberment of this complicated series of agreements. The new leadership in Germany, unwilling to understand or follow the logic of Bismarck's policies, turned aside Russian eagerness to renew the Reinsurance Treaty. As a result, the Treaty was allowed to lapse in 1890.

From the mid-1880s, these numerous alliances influenced the relative dependence of our dyads. In the middle of the decade, Germany/Austria-Hungary was by far the dominant dependent dyad. Next, though far behind, came Germany/Italy and Austria-Hungary/Italy. The last allied dyads at the mid-decade included Germany/Russia and Russia/Austria. As the decade's end approached, these rankings began to change, with greater differentiation in dependence among the dyads created by the Mediterranean agreements. In 1886-1888, Germany/Austria-Hungary remained the dominant dyad, followed by Germany/Italy and Austria-Hungary/Italy, and Germany/Russia. Russia/Austria-Hungary, by this time, was already ranked behind Britain/Austria-Hungary, Britain/Italy, and Germany/Britain. Given these changes, we would expect to see that Russia/Austria's symmetry levels should increase, while dyads with Britain, excluding Russia and France, would be related to lower symmetry rankings.

The signing of the Second Mediterranean Agreement alters the rankings once again. The last time period finds that Germany/Italy is now the most dependent dyad, followed by Germany/Austria-Hungary, Austria-Hungary/Italy, Britain/Austria-Hungary, and Britain/Italy. This last period reveals also the rupture between Russia and Austria-Hungary. There are no alliance-months for Russia/Austria-Hungary at all. Russia/Austria-Hungary is now ranked with dyads including France that formed no alliances with any powers in the entire twenty-one–year period. As a consequence of these changes in alliance, we should find Russian and French dyads, by the end of the decade, related to our highest symmetry of behavior rankings. Dyads with Italy, Austria-Hungary, Britain, and Germany should be related to the lower ranks of behavioral symmetry.

TABLE 5.7   Paired Comparisons: Alliance and Symmetry

	Symmetry of Cooperation		Symmetry of Conflict	
1870-73*	-		-	
1873-75	0		50	
1874-76	29		75	
1875-77	50		50	
1876-78	41		27	
1877-79	71		29	
1878-80	57		47	
1879-81	-		-	
1880-82	83		18	
1881-83	30		13	
1882-84	54		35	
1883-85	57		36	
1884-86	52		29	
1885-87	55		36	
1886-88	57		22	
1887-89	67		38	
1888-90	42		8	
Percentage of time periods that confirm the Alliance Hypothesis	2/15	12%	7/15	47%
Percentage of time periods that confirm the opposite of the Alliance Hypothesis	2/15	12%	1/15	7%

*The first time period includes an extra year due to lack of interactions.

**Above 70 percent is regarded as significant; below 30 percent is regarded as significant.

Table 5.7 presents the results of the Alliance Hypothesis.[19] In contrast to previous findings, we note relatively strong support for at least a part of the hypothesis. Though our findings are not significant, we recognize that there are a number of instances where the symmetry of conflict and alliance are related in the manner hypothesized (see Table 5.8 for all individual dyad comparisons).

Of our dyads, Germany/Austria-Hungary, Germany/Russia, Russia/Austria-Hungary, Austria-Hungary/Italy, and Germany/

Italy are the most allied, while Germany/Britain, Britain/Austria-Hungary, and Britain/Italy are allied but less so. Meanwhile, dyads like Germany/France, Russia/Britain, Britain/France, and Russia/France are totally independent. Looking more closely at the results of the analysis, once again, Germany/Austria-Hungary appears to affect our findings negatively, particularly with cooperation.

Germany/Austria-Hungary has a symmetry of cooperation too high for the highly allied position it finds itself in from 1873 through 1890. Though Austria-Hungary's alignment declines relatively after the mid-1880s, its behavior is far too highly symmetric for what remains a very allied pair of states. In conflict symmetry, the poor findings relate again to this same high symmetry of behavior for a very allied dyad. It is only extremely high conflict rankings displayed by independent dyads Germany/France and Russia/Britain which show strong confirmations of the Alliance Hypothesis with Germany/Austria-Hungary.

Germany/Austria-Hungary alone does not refute our hypothesis. Germany/Britain is another dyad which displays frequent lack of support for our hypothesis. For most of these two decades, Germany/Britain is an independent dyad. Yet it is evident in comparing it with all dependent dyads that Germany/Britain has far too low a symmetry of both cooperation and conflict for a largely independent dyad. Certainly, referring to our rankings of symmetry for various time periods (Appendix B), particularly after the Berlin Conference, the rankings of symmetry, particularly conflict, are low. Several factors account for this: there is Germany's refusal to proceed with talks on closer relations with Great Britain after first suggesting such talks. There are the occasional suggestions by Bismarck regarding Egypt which are turned away by the British. Finally, there are discreet German inquiries in regard to British colonial possessions in southwest Africa which result in British claims to control vast territories. These interactions over colonial issues result in lower symmetry levels in the 1880s. A return to higher

TABLE 5.8 Individual Dyad Comparisons of the Alliance Hypothesis

	Ger/Rus	Ger/Frn	Ger/Aus	Ger/Itl	Brt/Rus	Brt/Frn	Brt/Aus	Brt/Itl	Rus/Frn	Rus/Aus	Rus/Itl	Frn/Aus	Frn/Itl	Aus/Itl
Ger/Brt	36 46 / 14 13	33 100 / 3 3	0 33 / 13 9	29 43 / 7 7	100 100 / 2 2	50 75 / 4 4	0 100 / 2 2	25 100 / 4 1	25 0 / 4 4	27 36 / 11 11	– – / – –	· ·	· ·	75 43 / 8 7
Ger/Rus	Ger/Rus	69 90 / 13 10	55 18 / 11 11	44 50 / 9 8	73 73 / 11 11	38 89 / 13 9	20 0 / 10 3	29 25 / 7 4	4 4 / 50 50	50 50 / 4 6	– –	· ·	· ·	55 50 / 11 8
Ger/Frn		Ger/Frn	42 86 / 12 7	60 75 / 5 4	– – / – –	– – / – –	33 100 / 3 3	0 – / 3 3	8 8 / 50 50	73 56 / 11 9	– –	· ·	0 100 / 3 3	60 100 / 5 4
Ger/Aus			Ger/Aus	0 43 / 8 7	20 100 / 10 8	36 50 / 11 8	0 0 / 3 3	0 33 / 6 3	0 4 / 6 0	44 67 / 9 9	– –	3 –	67 100 / 3 3	6 25 / 8 8
Ger/Itl				Ger/Itl	100 75 / 4 4	43 57 / 7 7	10 0 / 3 3	75 3 / 4 –	25 4 / 4 –	67 50 / 6 6	– –	100 0 / 3 1	100 100 / 1 1	0 0 / 3 2
Brt/Rus					Brt/Rus	– – / – –	0 100 / 3 3	100 100 / 2 2	0 3 / 0 3	75 78 / 8 9	– –	· ·	· ·	100 100 / 3 5
Brt/Frn						Brt/Frn	100 – / 4 3	33 100 / 3 1	0 3 / 3 0	29 17 / 7 6	– –	· ·	· ·	71 100 / 7 6
Brt/Aus							Brt/Aus	3 – / 3 –	0 1 / 3 –	13 67 / 8 3	– –	100 0 / 3 1	0 0 / 3 3	100 0 / 4 3
Brt/Itl								Brt/Itl	· ·	8 0 / 4 3	– –	· ·	0 3 / 3 3	75 100 / 4 1
Rus/Frn									Rus/Frn	20 0 / 5 6	– –	· ·	· ·	50 0 / 4 3
Rus/Aus										Rus/Aus	– –	100 0 / 3 1	· ·	88 88 / 8 8
Rus/Itl											Rus/Itl	· ·	· ·	· ·
Frn/Aus												Frn/Aus	· ·	100 1 / · ·
Frn/Itl													Frn/Itl	100 50 / 1 2
														Aus/Itl

Abbreviations: Ger = Germany, Brt = Britain, Rus = Russia, Aus = Austria-Hungary, Frn = France, Itl = Italy.

Symmetry of Cooperation ┐ Symmetry of Conflict ┐

Percentage	x	x = Percentage
Number	xx	xx = Number

116

symmetry does not take place until after the initial colonial skirmishes are over. At that point, the symmetry of conflict increases, particularly the directed dyad Britain/Germany: Britain's demands over colonial territories are rejected. After 1885, the directed dyad Germany/Britains' conflict symmetry increases although the conflict symmetry declines by the end of the 1880s. This symmetry decline toward the end of the 1880s is helpful. As Britain and Germany sign or adhere to the Mediterranean accords, the symmetry of conflict declines, as our hypothesis would suggest.

However, this declining pattern with the Mediterranean agreements is not consistently evident. We argued earlier that dyads influenced by the Mediterranean agreements, including Germany/Britain, Austria-Hungary/Britain, and Britain/Italy, should experience a reduction in their behavioral symmetry ranks. But examining the cooperation symmetries for all three dyads, one notices that the levels of symmetry actually increase. Thus, we are made aware how difficult it is to relate the changes in alliance to rapidly varying behavior changes.

The pattern of confirmation of the Alliance Hypothesis is very confused. There are independent dyads like Germany/France and Russia/Britain that support the Alliance Hypothesis, and others such as Russia/France or Britain/France that do not. There are dependent dyads like Austria-Hungary/Italy and Germany/Russia that confirm, largely, the Alliance Hypothesis, and others like Austria-Hungary/Germany and Austria-Hungary/Russia that do not.

Of the two behavior patterns, cooperation appears to be more complicated than conflict. If one places all the dyads along the alliance continuum, the high symmetry of cooperation rankings cuts across alliance types. It is evident that both Germany/France or Russia/Britain, highly independent dyads, and Germany/Austria-Hungary, a highly dependent or allied dyad, have high rankings of symmetry of cooperation. Our Alliance Hypothesis argued that the more dependent the dyad was, the lower the symmetries of behavior. While some cases follow this pattern—e.g., Austria-Hungary/Italy—we do not find a consistent pattern for our allied dyads. In fact, there appears to be a paradox. Both dependent allied, and independent unallied dyads exhibit high symmetry levels of cooperation. This "paradox of cooperation" helps to explain the failure to confirm the Alliance Hypothesis and likely our other structural hypotheses with the symmetry of cooperation and total symmetry. It does not explain how, or if, our structural hypotheses can be confirmed. Alliance, like power and then status and status inconsistency, is not related systematically to the symmetry of interaction as the Alliance Hypothesis suggested. Once again, the analysis is unable to relate consistently a structural variable to the logic of diplomacy.

So far, none of our structural indicators have confirmed our hypotheses. Power, status, and alliance have not revealed a relationship with actor interaction—symmetry. But our closer dyadic analysis—with alliance, and with power and status—indicated that a reanalysis of the individual dyads might offer further understanding of the relationship of our structural indicators and diplomatic activity. In the next chapter, we shall take a closer and more discrete look at individual dyads, their patterns of interaction, and power, status, and alliance characteristics, and try and give an explanation for the failure of the structural variables to explain the variations in the symmetry of behavior.

NOTES

1. David Baldwin (1971a, 1971b, 1971c), in his writing on the influence process has noted the importance of costs. As he argued (1971a: 147): "The main point of including costs in the concept of power, however, is to deny that power is solely a matter of effectiveness. The point is to assert that power should be conceived and measured in terms of both cost and effectiveness."

2. In a study of the influence process, Leng (1980: 129-130) established hypotheses whose logics seem to closely parallel that described here.

3. Attributes suggested here consist only of objective qualities. Subjective factors include the quality of leadership, the efficiency of administration, patriotism, and other qualities not easily susceptible to measurement. As difficult as it is to agree completely on the means of defining and measuring power objectively, this task pales

in comparison to the same task with subjective power. Even if it were possible to come to some agreement on what subjective power should include, the question of how to measure subjective power would remain a significant dilemma for the researcher. As a result, this analysis has restricted itself to defining valid indicators of objective power. But for a wide-ranging discussion of the various measurements of both subjective and objective power, see Knorr (1975).

4. A review of the major projects reveals the consistency of dimensions though it shows a wide variety of variables used within those dimensions.

The Correlates of War has settled on six indicators of power—total population, urban population, military expenditures, military personnel, iron and steel production, and energy consumption (Singer et al., 1972: 26). They have suggested these six indicators represent the major facets of attribute power.

The Situational Analysis Project (Rosecrance et al., 1974: 13) created a twenty-five indicator power index representing seven dimensions—military, demographic, fiscal, economic, trade, education, and financial. Rosecrance et al. (1974: 11) argued that these seven dimensions covered the major facets of objective power.

Choucri and North (1975), whose recent research focuses on national growth and conflict, employed various indicators of objective power, including dimensions of technology, military capabilities, economic productivity, commercial activity, and a budget dimension.

Wayne Ferris's study (1973) of power capabilities focuses more closely on power which has direct sanctioning capability. Nevertheless, most of his indicators overlap with other research projects. Ferris's indicators include area, population logged, government revenues per capita, and defense expenditure per capita.

Finally, the Dimensionality of Nations Project has collected many power indicators. Possibly the most complex project of all, this research has employed large matrices of power. Two major dimensions have consistently appeared—economic development and military power (Rummel, 1971).

5. Though the analysis of power has been as broad as possible, ultimately the scope of power becomes an analytic problem. Other indicators of power could be included; the balance between military and industrial dimensions could be altered; even the indicators could be combined in a variety of ways other than those examined here. No definition of power is completely acceptable. Nevertheless, the analysis has taken pains to remain thorough. The indicators of power—except possibly for revenue per capita—were chosen because of their historical influence on decision makers. Moreover, the analysis has tested not only indexes but the influence of all individual indicators with symmetry. Thus, various arrangements of our European powers have been tested and not those limited to the index arrangements. The breadth of testing increases our confidence that attribute power has been examined fully in regard to actor interaction.

6. There is no consensus on the relative importance of the variables. Historians (Schroeder, 1977) and political scientists (Ferris, 1973) frequently argue that military power should be weighted more heavily than other dimensions, or that the list should be pared to add weight to the military dimension because military power is more immediate and more directly sanctioning. Ferris (1973), for instance, in a novel approach, weighted the indicators by their factor loadings. Rather than bias the categories in ways that are not theoretically grounded, we have decided to weight the variables equally.

7. Germany is always a difficult case to assess, for on objective power measures it appears to come out lower than it should. For an argument which suggests that Germany's ranking reflects the realities of power at the time, see Alexandroff et al. (1977: 47-52).

8. William Blackwell (1970: 23), writing on the development of the Russian economy, puts it this way: "Nevertheless, a remarkable economic growth took place in Russia during the last decades of the Tsarist regime. By the eve of the Great War, Russia was the world's fifth industrial power. In terms of strict economic measurement, rapid industrialization began no earlier than the mid-1880's."

9. For a complete description of the methods and arguments for their use, see the Appendix A.

10. The individual dyad comparisons over time use the same significance levels as the general analysis to confirm or disconfirm the hypothesized relationship between power and symmetry.

11. The initial paired-comparison tests were total dyad symmetry levels, which in fact are the combined stimuli and responses of both powers—each as actor and as target. Within the dyads, it is possible that the symmetry level may be biased substantially by widely different frequencies of actions on the part of either one of the powers as indicator. In order to check for this, the indexes and selected individual indicators were reanalyzed but in this case the symmetry levels were calcualted separately—these are directed dyads. Then the two symmetries were added together and the total was divided by two, providing a combined symmetry (total dyad) where the influence of initiations by each directed dyad was exactly equal to the other. The findings were not significantly altered, however.

12. Rummel's argument for excluding prestige relies partly on theoretical grounds and partly on methodological grounds. Status field theory defines status dimensions as linearly independent (he provides a methodological definition for this). Both economic development and power are linearly independent. Esteem or prestige, however, is not independent; instead, prestige is dependent on economic development and power, and therefore it is excluded as a dimension of status.

13. The dissociative (conflictual) pattern is simply the mirror image of the associative patterns seen in the Cooperation Hypothesis.

14. The maximum period shows these three actor types—TT, UU, and TU. The result is TT-TT, TT-TU, UU-UU, and UU-TU.

15. This decision to weight one form of alliance seems a little at variance with the earlier decision on power, but there are several reasons for this. For one thing, there is a consensus on the greater commitment of defense pacts while there remain questions as to what defines power. Also, there are far fewer categories to decide between whereas we have seen with power that the range of possible indicators is quite large.

16. The best source for identifying alliances from 1870-1890 is Singer and Small (1966). But the list is incomplete and further assistance can be obtained by Langer (1950).

17. In order to capture the greater commitments of defense pacts, we multiply the number of alliance-months by 1.0. For the remainder of the agreements we multiply the total alliance-months by 0.5. Somewhat arbitrarily, we have weighted the alliance-months twice that of either neutrality or entente alliance. But even at 0.8, the ranks we create remain identical. Partly because of the uncertainty of the weighting, ordinal measurements appear the most appropriate means of comparison.

18. There can be no adequate detailing of the works on Bismarck here. For some representative views of him and more complete biographies, see Eyck, 1950; Geiss, 1976; Hamerow, 1972; Kissinger, 1968; Langer, 1950; Medlicott, 1965; Pflanze, 1976; Rohl, 1970; Taylor, 1955/1967; Waller, 1974; Wehler, 1970.

19. In this table, a rating below 30 percent confirms the Alliance Hypothesis for the symmetry of cooperation and the symmetry of conflict. A rating above 70 percent for all three patterns confirms the opposite of the Alliance Hypothesis.

Chapter 6

REINTERPRETING STRUCTURAL EXPLANATIONS

A SECOND LOOK AT
THE STRUCTURAL VARIABLES

Chapter Five revealed quite dramatically the failure of structural variables to explain the variations in diplomatic interactions. Individual cases, it is true, confirmed certain structural hypotheses, yet overall these explanations were not consistently confirmed by the data. The task is to explain the failure of these structural hypotheses and to determine where the explanation for our results lies.

To accomplish this task we have reanalyzed the data (both for illustrative and comparative purposes), simplifying the symmetry patterns. In this analysis symmetry is measured every five years and categorized as either high or low.[1] Similarly, we have also simplified the structural attributes to give a comprehensive yet more manageable picture of all the dyads.[2]

Categorizing our patterns of symmetry as either high or low, four distinct types of behavioral symmetry emerge (see Table

6.1)—two cooperative or associative symmetry patterns and two relatively conflictual or dissociative symmetry patterns.[3] Along the bottom of Table 6.1 we identify the two associative or cooperative patterns: along the top the two dissociative patterns are located. The two types of behavior along the bottom define non threat-counterthreat patterns—both include low conflict symmetry. The two dissociative behavior types, containing threat-counterthreat interactions, are defined along the top.

The Alliance Hypothesis argued that allied dyads would exhibit the associative patterns of symmetry while independent dyads would display the dissociative ones. Of the type just described, allied dyads should have exhibited collegial patterns (associative), while independent dyads should have revealed competitive patterns (dissociative).

For power, it was argued that more equal powers would exhibit dissociative patterns of symmetry (competitive), while less equal power dyads would reveal more associative patterns of symmetry (collegial).

For status inconsistency, we hypothesized that topdog states or underdog states or topdog and underdog states which were also status inconsistent would reveal cooperative patterns of symmetry. In this case the collaborative pattern was the associa-

TABLE 6.1   Symmetry Patterns—Behavior Types

		COOPERATION SYMMETRY		
		HIGH	LOW	
CONFLICTUAL SYMMETRY	HIGH	Competitive	Antagonistic	DISSOCIATIVE
	LOW	Collaborative	Collegial	ASSOCIATIVE

NOTE: The four behavior type names are intended to differentiate relatively cooperative from relatively conflictual patterns. They are not used to compare between like types. Therefore, competitive and antagonistic patterns indicate no difference in the level of dissociative behavior nor does collaborative or collegial patterns indicate associative behavior patterns. They provide a useful descriptive labeling function only.

tive pattern identified. Topdog and underdog states that were relatively status inconsistent were hypothesized to be related to dissociative patterns, in this case the antagonistic pattern.

Analytically defining two types of associative and dissociative behaviors, one notes an immediate problem for our previous structural hypotheses. In each of our structural hypotheses, we have suggested one pattern of cooperative and conflictual symmetry for our dyads, yet logically there are at least two. This should account partly for our limited findings.

EXPLAINING ALLIANCE, POWER, STATUS INCONSISTENCY, AND SYMMETRY

Table 6.2 displays the patterns of symmetry and identifies the dyadic behavior types over the twenty-one years. Some dyads are not identified for all four periods because they did not have a complete set of cooperative and conflictual symmetry patterns. Remember that our associative/dissociative patterns are a combination of cooperative and conflictual symmetry.

The placement of the dyads reveals some interesting confirmations and disconfirmations of our structural hypotheses.

As we noted, our hypotheses were so constructed that confirmation of these hypotheses required our dyads to display a single pattern of associative and dissociative behavior. For power and alliance, our less equal powers and our allied dyads were required to exhibit low conflict and low cooperative symmetry, according to the high/low symmetry categorization. At the other structural extreme, independent dyads and more equal power dyads were to display high conflict symmetry and high cooperation symmetry. For status and status inconsistency, single patterns of cooperation and conflict symmetry were also required to obtain a confirmation of our hypothesis.

But as Table 6.2 shows, such is not the case. While allied dyad Germany/Russia reveals a collegial pattern, it also displays the alternative associative pattern—collaboration. Thus, Ger-

TABLE 6.2   Behavior Types—Five Year Breakdown of Dyads*

COOPERATION SYMMETRY

		HIGH		LOW	
CONFLICT SYMMETRY	HIGH	Germany/Britain	1	Germany/Britain	3
		Germany/France	2 (3)→4	Germany/Russia	2
		Germany/Aus-Hun	4	Germany/France	1
		France/Italy	3	Russia/Aus-Hun	(2)←
		Britain/Russia	2 3 4	France/Italy	4
		Britain/France	4		
		Russia/Aus-Hun	(1)↓3 4		
	LOW	Germany/Britain	2 (4)→	Germany/Russia	(1)←(4)↑
		Germany/Russia	3	Germany/Italy	3
		Germany/Aus-Hun	2 (3)→	Aus-Hun/Italy	3 4
		Germany/Italy	(4)	Russia/France	2
		Russia/France	4	Britain/Italy	2
		France/Aus-Hun	2	France/Aus-Hun	3
		Britain/Russia	1		
		Britain/France	3		
		Britain/Aus-Hun	4		
		Britain/Italy	4		

*Numbers denote time periods: 1. 1870-1874; 2. 1875-1879; 3. 1880-1884;
4. 1885-1890. Numbers in parentheses indicate an ambiguous categorization.
The arrows following these numbers point to the alternate descriptive pattern
possible given the rather crude categorization of symmetry.

many/Russia maintains associative patterns of interaction, but
patterns which would only partly confirm our original hypothesis. Equally, Germany/Italy, an unequal power dyad, exhibits a symmetry of cooperation and conflict helping to confirm
the Power Hypothesis. Yet it also reveals a collaborative pattern
of high cooperation and low conflict symmetry. The pattern of
interaction is still associative but the pattern would partly
disconfirm the Power Hypothesis.

At the other extreme of alliance and power, the same mixed
pattern is evident. The Alliance Hypothesis required independent dyad Germany/France to possess a pattern of high cooperation symmetry and high conflict symmetry to confirm the

relationship of alliance and symmetry of behavior. While Germany/France exhibits this competitive behavior type, it also reveals the alternative dissociative pattern—high conflict symmetry and low cooperation symmetry. And Germany/France as a more equal power dyad reveals the identical mixed dissociative patterns. Once again, while the dyad displays the correct category of behavior—dissociative—Germany/France partly disproves the Alliance and Power Hypotheses.

Finally, status and status inconsistency call for patterns of either antagonistic or collaborative behavior, depending on the type of status or status inconsistency of the dyads; yet the same mixed pattern of associative and dissociative behavior appears. Relatively, status-consistent topdog/underdog France/Austria exhibits the appropriate associative behavior type—high cooperation and low conflict symmetry—but it also shows low cooperation, low conflict symmetry. Status-inconsistent topdog/underdog France/Italy reveals a dissociative pattern of high conflict symmetry and low cooperation symmetry but also a pattern of high cooperation and high conflict symmetry. Thus, dyads exhibiting dual patterns of associative and dissociative behavior explain the inability of our structural hypothesis to be confirmed strongly.

The difficulties in confirming our hypotheses do not end with the problem of dual associative patterns. Table 6.3 reveals a much more serious disconfirming mixture of cases. This table contrasts allied dyads with independent dyads. It shows that not only do allied dyads show both associative patterns—collaborative and collegial—but that allied dyads also display both competitive and antagonistic dissociative patterns. Not only are both dissociative patterns evident with our independent dyads, but associative dyads appear as well.

Table 6.4 focuses on the allied dyads during the greater part of these twenty-one years—Germany/Russia, Germany/Austria-Hungary, and Russia/Austria-Hungary. A comparison of our behavior types reveals deeply contrasting patterns. While Germany/Austria-Hungary maintains a largely collaborative pattern, it displays a competitive pattern in the final period. Germany/

TABLE 6.3   Alliance and Behavioral Types*

Allied

COOPERATION SYMMETRY

		HIGH	LOW	
CONFLICT SYMMETRY	HIGH	Russia/Aus-Hun (1) 3 4 Germany/Aus-Hun 4	Germany/Russia 2 Russia/Aus-Hun 2	DIS-SOCIA-TIVE
	LOW	Germany/Russia 3 Germany/Aus-Hun 2 (3) Germany/Italy 4 Britain/Italy 4 Britain/Aus-Hun 4 Germany/Britain 4	Germany/Russia (1) (4) Germany/Italy 3 Aus-Hun/Italy 3 4	ASSO-CIA-TIVE

Independent

COOPERATION SYMMETRY

		HIGH	LOW	
CONFLICT SYMMETRY	HIGH	Britain/Russia 2 3 4 Germany/France 2 (3) 4 France/Italy 3	Germany/France 1 France/Italy 4	DIS-SOCIA-TIVE
	LOW	Britain/Russia 1 Russia/France 4 France/Aus-Hun 2 Germany/Britain 2	Russia/France 2 France/Aus-Hun 3 Britain/Italy 2	ASSO-CIA-TIVE

*Numbers indicate time periods: 1. 1870-1874; 2. 1875-1879; 3. 1880-1884; 4. 1885-1890. Numbers in parentheses indicate ambiguous categorizations.

Russia displays both a collaborative pattern and a collegial pattern. Like Germany/Austria-Hungary, Germany/Russia displays a dissociative pattern. Most revealing is Russia/Austria-Hungary. This dyad fails to show an associative pattern at all. The behavior types demonstrate that the relationships between these various powers are not similar, though the patterns of alliance little distinguish among these dyads.

The distinctions built into our alliances—military, entente, neutrality—are general and have provided some variations in the degree of "alliedness" of our allied dyads; yet these distinctions

TABLE 6.4 The Behavior Types: Three Emperors' League, Three Emperors' Alliance plus Dual Alliance and Reinsurance Treaty*

Allied

COOPERATION SYMMETRY

		HIGH	LOW	
CONFLICT SYMMETRY	HIGH	Russia/Aus-Hun (1) 3 4 Germany/Aus-Hun 4	Germany/Russia 2 Russia/Aus-Hun (2)	DIS-SOCIA-TIVE
	LOW	Germany/Russia 3 Germany/Aus-Hun 2 (3)	Germany/Russia (1) (4)	ASSO-CIA-TIVE

Independent

COOPERATION SYMMETRY

		HIGH	LOW	
CONFLICT SYMMETRY	HIGH	Britain/Russia 2 3 4 Germany/France 2 (3) 4 France/Italy 3	Germany/France 1 France/Italy 4	DIS-SOCIA-TIVE
	LOW	Britain/Russia 1 Britain/France 3 Russia/France 4 France/Aus-Hun 2	Russia/France 2 France/Aus-Hun 3 France/Italy 2	ASSO-CIA-TIVE

*Numbers indicate time periods: 1. 1870-1874; 2. 1875-1879; 3. 1880-1884; 4. 1885-1890. Numbers in parentheses indicate ambiguous categorizations.

have missed differences, particularly in the way alliances were used in the Bismarckian system. The Bismarckian alliances affected the system of powers in at least two ways in these twenty-one years. One type of alliance seems to have joined together parties against a common external actor or actors. This alliance type exacerbated the polarity of the system of states. The Dual Alliance, for example, focused on Russia, the Triple Alliance on Russia and France.

Yet alliances appear to have been concluded in these years to bridge differences and diffuse polarities in the system. Thus, the Three Emperors' League appears to have been established to formalize common ground between potentially conflicting powers. Russia and Austria-Hungary saw each other as rivals in the Balkans; Bismarck went to great diplomatic effort to keep these two eastern monarchies from forcing Germany to choose between them over the conflicts of interest in the Balkans.

Besides the contrasting external uses that alliances were put to in these years, alliances also served different internal purposes. Alliances were used on the one hand to support alliance partners. Italy and Austria-Hungary were both strengthened by their agreements with Germany in the early 1880s. The Mediterranean Agreements appear to have provided mutual support among Italy, Austria and Britain. On the other hand, particularly for Bismarck, alliances were used to restrain the activities of members of the agreement. By calling on ties created by these agreements, Bismarck appears to have limited Austria-Hungary in the Balkans.

These alliance uses, both external and internal, may well influence the patterns of interactions of the alliance partners and possibly some actors outside the alliances as well. Because externally oriented agreements focus attention outside the group and provide external support, they may well be related to associative behavior patterns. Bridging agreements because they include antagonists are more likely to be related to dissociative patterns of interaction. Also, alliances which constrain partners are more likely to see competitive and antagonistic patterns of symmetry.

Can these distinctions help to clarify the mixed symmetry patterns among Germany, Russia, and Austria-Hungary? Turning to our most exceptional case, Russia/Austria-Hungary, we see that "alliance-use"[4] distinctions help us in explaining the failure to see associative patterns of behavior. Russia and Austria-Hungary were linked together through the Three Emperors' League and the Alliance. For Russia/Austria-Hungary there were no rivals more evident than each other, largely because of the Balkans. The dissociative patterns of symmetry suggest that the rivalry remained evident even given the attempted alliances. The bridging Bismarck envisioned failed to materialize. According to our alliance data, however, these two powers had become relatively highly allied.

Turning to Germany/Austria-hungary, the patterns of inter-action are much changed from this former case. "Alliance use" can be helpful here in explaining the exceptional symmetry patterns. The earlier periods correspond to expected patterns; they are both associative. However, the last time period displays a competitive pattern of interaction. Furthermore, in Chapter Five, the general alliance analysis, it was found that Germany/Austria-Hungary's symmetry levels ranked highly, though the dyad was the most allied for almost the entire twenty-one years. This relatively high level might reflect the mixed nature of Germany/Austria-Hungary's alliances. While the alliance-month totals do not distinguish between different alliance purposes, Germany/Austria-Hungary's commitments include both polariz-ing alliances such as the Dual Alliance and bridging agreements such as the Three Emperors' Alliance. Moreover, Bismarck used the alliances as much to constrain partners as to support them. In the last period, as a result of the Balkan imbroglio between Austria-Hungary and Russia, Bismarck was forced to restrain Austria-Hungary in its threats against Russia. The German/Aus-trian ties enabled Bismarck to warn Austria-Hungary that haste in the Balkans would leave it without German support. This pressure on Austria-Hungary, using the alliance to constrain Austrian efforts, is reflected in the competitive pattern of symmetry of Germany/Austria-Hungary.

Finally, our alliance distinctions may explain the distinctive patterns of symmetry with Germany/Russia as well. The late 1870s were perceived by Russia as a period when Germany failed to support Russian efforts. Bismarck aided efforts to control Russia's Balkan gains. The Congress of Berlin turned Gorchakov and the Tsar into bitter Bismarckian critics. The dissociative pattern of symmetry of Germany/Russia certainly reflects both this lack of support and the failure to straddle Russian and Austrian objectives in this difficult period. In the late 1880s Germany/Russia signed the Reinsurance Treaty, an alliance nominally pointed against external adversaries. In contrast to previous agreements between Germany/Russia, Austria-Hungary is excluded from this 1887 agreement. The period exhibits an associative pattern of symmetry, much as we would expect from "alliance-use" distinctions.

These alliance distinctions also help to suggest the associative behavior types exhibited by all the Mediterranean Agreement partners. The Mediterranean Agreements directed at Russia and France encouraged associative patterns for Germany/Britain, Germany/Italy, Britain/Italy, and Britain/Austria-Hungary. Focusing on actors outside the agreements and lending support to cosigners, these agreements help to confirm the Alliance Hypothesis. All allied dyads are related to associative behavior patterns.

Some of the exceptions in the independent dyads might be accounted for by "alliance use". In terms of alliance formation in these twenty-one years, France and Russia both appear to be the main targets of externally directed agreements. The marked associative patterns of symmetry by this dyad may well reflect their mutually isolated position. The associative patterns of behavior of these two isolated states were capped by formal commitments not long after 1890. The 1891 August Convention, the forerunner of the Russo-French Entente, seems to have confirmed these earlier associative behavioral patterns.[5]

Introducing distinctions in alliance purpose has helped to further our explanation of the relationship of alliance to patterns of symmetry. These distinctions have partly corrected the crude alliance calculations. As a result, the analysis has been able to explain the mixed patterns of association with alliance. Both alliance and "alliance use" seem necessary to relate alliance differences and patterns of association.

, Turning to Table 6.5, we see the relationship of behavior types and the dyads differentiated by more or less equal power. Just as with alliances, power differences exhibit mixed patterns of associative and dissociative behavior. While the Power Hypothesis suggested that more equal power dyads would be related to dissociative patterns of symmetry, there are a number of more equal power dyads that display collaborative and collegial

TABLE 6.5   Combined Power and Behavior Types*

More Equal Power Dyads

COOPERATION SYMMETRY

		HIGH		LOW		
CONFLICT SYMMETRY	HIGH	Germany/France Russia/Aus-Hun	2 (3) 4 (1) 3 4	Germany/France 1 Germany/Russia 2 Russia/Aus-Hun 2		DIS- SOCIA- TIVE
	LOW	Germany/Russia Germany/Aus-Hun Russia/France France/Aus-Hun	3 2 4 2	Aus-Hun/Italy 3 4 Germany/Russia (1) (4) Russia/France 2 France/Aus-Hun 3		ASSO- CIA- TIVE

Less Equal Power Dyads

COOPERATION SYMMETRY

		HIGH		LOW		
CONFLICT SYMMETRY	HIGH	Germany/Britain Britain/Russia Germany/Aus-Hun France/Italy Britain/France	1 2 3 4 4 3 4	Germany/Britain 3 France/Italy 4		DIS- SOCIA- TIVE
	LOW	Germany/Britain Britain/Russia Britain/Italy Britain/Aus-Hun Germany/Aus-Hun Germany/Italy Britain/France	2 (4) 1 4 4 (3) (4) 3	Britain/Italy 2 Germany/Italy 3		ASSO- CIA- TIVE

*Numbers indicate time periods: 1. 1870-1874; 2. 1875-1879; 3. 1880-1884; 4. 1885-1890. Numbers in parentheses indicate ambiguous categorizations.

patterns of symmetry. Though numerous less equal power dyads exhibit associative patterns of symmetry, as the Power Hypothesis suggested, there are cases of less equal power dyads that display both competitive and antagonistic patterns of symmetry.

What explains the mixture of associative and dissociative behavior patterns with our power differences? If we focus on more equal power dyads, particularly those exhibiting associative patterns, it appears that aside from France/Austria-Hungary, all these dyad cases have been discussed in the previous alliance case. These dyads suggest the dominant influence of alliance differences on these more equal power dyads. This influence is not surprising. The analysis has argued alliances' more closely political nature and correspondingly more difficult role on patterns of interaction. The equal power cases in the associative categories of behavior lend support to this view.

Turning to the unequal power cases, we find that many of these dyads are related to associative behavior patterns. Still, there are dyadic exceptions. Germany/Austria-Hungary has been discussed with alliance and "alliance-use" distinctions. But unexplained cases include Germany/Britain, Britain/Russia, France/Italy, and Britain/France. One of the most evident similarities among these unequal power dyads is the fact that all these dyads except Germany/Britain were involved in serious colonial disputes in the 1870-1874 period. These dyads all have competitive or antagonistic patterns of interaction. The Power Hypothesis argued that unequal power dyads were more likely to exhibit associative patterns of behavior. In these unequal power cases, colonial tensions have intervened and the patterns of behavior have become predominantly competitive. From this behavioral perspective colonial issues appear to have raised tensions in the system of European states.[6]

While colonial disputes are helpful in explaining some of our exceptions, they do not provide a more general unnderstanding of why unequal powers are more often engaged in colonial disputes; it narrows our explanation of the relationship of power differences and symmetry to unique historical events. Nonetheless, the intervening alliance patterns and colonial conflicts help us to understand further the mixed patterns of symmetry and the failure of power to relate significantly to symmetry.

The table on status inconsistency and behavior types (Table 6.6) appears to contain the most mixed pattern of attribute dyads. In fact, the exceptional cases are so evident and numerous that status inconsistency appears less open to further expla-

TABLE 6.6   Status Inconsistency and Behavior Types*

Topdogs and Underdogs, Topdogs or Underdogs – Consistent

COOPERATION SYMMETRY

		HIGH		LOW		
CONFLICT SYMMETRY	HIGH	Russia/Aus-Hun Germany/France Germany/Britain Britain/France	(1) 3 4 2 (3) 4 1 4	Russia/Australia Germany/France Germany/Britain	2 1 3	DIS- SOCIA- TIVE
	LOW	Germany/Britain Britain/France France/Aus-Hun	2 (4) 3 2	Aus-Hun/Italy France/Aus-Hun	3 4 3	ASSO- CIA- TIVE

Topdogs and Underdogs – Inconsistent

COOPERATION SYMMETRY

		HIGH		LOW		
CONFLICT SYMMETRY	HIGH	Germany/Aus-Hun Britain/Russia France/Italy	4 2 3 4 3	Germany/Russia France/Italy	2 4	DIS- SOCIA- TIVE
	LOW	Germany/Aus-Hun Britain/Russia Russia/France Germany/Russia Britain/Italy Britain/Aus-Hun Germany/Italy	2 (3) 1 4 3 4 4 4	Russia/France Germany/Russia Britain/Italy Germany/Italy	2 1 4 2 3	ASSO- CIA TIVE

*Numbers indicate time periods: 1. 1870-1874; 2. 1875-1879; 3. 1880-1884; 4. 1885-1890. Numbers in parentheses indicate ambiguous categorizations.

nation. The large number of contrary cases, particularly with our inconsistent dyads, demonstrate that status inconsistency is poorly related to patterns of symmetry. Moreover, many of our prominent cases appear to contradict the Status-Inconsistency Hypothesis. In particular, the status theory notion that high-status states exhibit more associative patterns of behavior is seriously contradicted by Germany/France. Equally, the view that relatively consistent low-status states exhibit associative patterns of symmetry is belied by Russia/Austria-Hungary. Two exceptional cases, France/Italy and Britain/Russia provide a possible answer to our previous effort to explain why these two dyads, as unequal power dyads, exhibit conflictual symmetry patterns. Both dyads are status-inconsistent dyads. However, the extent of this explanation is modified by the fact that not all power cases can be explained by status-inconsistency distinctions. It suggests again the influence of one structural characteristic on another.

Our reanalysis has not given us a complete structural explanation of the variations in symmetry. Nevertheless, our examination of behavior types and the closer examination of the exceptions has suggested the interactive quality of the structural dimension that wasn't investigated in Chapter Five. Moreover, the analysis has added—through the notions of "alliance use" and colonial disputes—valuable distinctions that were missing from the simple structural categories. Particularly in the case of alliance, our closer examination has revealed the limitations of the definition of alliance. "Alliance use" has extended the structural variable's explanation of the logic of diplomacy. However, it does not provide a consistent explanation of the nature sought in Chapter Five.

The value of "alliance use" in contrast to alliance in explaining symmetry outcomes alerts us to the limitations of this important structural variable. It also suggests the need to now redefine alliance in a way more sensitive to the diplomacy of the powers if we hope to confirm a structural explanation of behavior. Our alliance variable was defined in formal terms only in Chapter Five. Yet in international politics there are frequently agreements of a far less formal kind. These agreements—what we will call alignments—usually consist of coordinated behavior or informal cooperative relations without formal treaties. Alignment lacks the commitment and the structured character of formal alliances, yet it may prove to be the more political and behavioral "structural" variable we need to explain variations in symmetry. Certainly alignment patterns are very evident in the period we are investigating even among independent or antagonistic states. Thus, while Germany and France are foes throughout these years, this does not exclude periods of more mutually aligned behavior. Indeed, in the early 1880s, Franco-German relations were marked by serious Bismarckian efforts to improve the diplomatic atmosphere between the two countries. This Franco-German entente directed the cooperative energies of the two states into colonial issues and against Great Britain. This alignment may have influenced the symmetry of the behavior of this dyad: no changes would be expected in symmetry from power, status, and alliance.

Another alignment case of longer standing is Great Britain and Austria-Hungary. These two countries maintained no formal ties with one another through most of our two decades. Both saw cooperation with each other as a useful objective. Britain and Austria shared a common foe—Russia. Once again, this informal link may well relate to the levels of symmetry of this dyad, while formal ties would not.

THE ALIGNMENT HYPOTHESIS

One of the difficulties in examining alignment is simply one of definition. Unlike alliance, alignment has no agreements capable of distinguishing the degree of dependence or independence, coordination or competition. And since we seek to measure alignment (which we suggest is a more behavioral form of alliance), we must be careful to distinguish it from our initial explanatory variable, which is behavior itself.

Various indicators were possible.[7] The most sensitive and most encompassing measure, and the one ultimately chosen, was one which incorporated the level of overall behavior between the various dyads. Alignment was defined as the amount of cooperation/conflict between the pairs of states, using once again the measurements of the Situational Analysis Project (Healy and Stein, 1973; Rosecrance et al., 1974). Our most aligned states will be those with the highest cooperation/conflict levels, our least aligned states those with the lowest level of behavior. In order to measure the levels of behavior, the Situational Analysis Data provides quantitatively measured actions that can be aggregated for a test of alignment over time.[8]

Hypothesis (Alignment Hypothesis)

The more cooperative the aggregate level of behavior between A and B, the higher the symmetry of cooperation and the lower the symmetry of conflict.

Table 6.7 reveals the results of the Alignment Hypothesis. We discover our first generally significant relationship between a structural indicator and symmetry of interaction. Indeed, in seven of our ten comparisons there is a significant relationship between alignment and symmetry of conflict across our dyads. The analysis indicates that the more aligned (measured by the aggregate level of cooperation/conflict) the dyads are, the lower symmetries of conflict; the less aligned the dyads are, the greater the symmetries of conflict. It is the short-term objectives and commitments—alignment—and not the more binding patterns of commitment (formal alliance) that explain conflict symmetry. And it is the more behavioral alignment, not the more structural power and status differences that help to explain the logic of diplomacy. Alignment, a structural attribute highly attuned to diplomatic activity, helps to explain in a consistent fashion the variations in symmetry among the powers. A comparison of alliance and alignment for selected dyads (see Table 6.8 for all the individual dyad comparisons) can highlight the difference of the formal and informal patterns of structure.

Of the dyads, only Germany/Austria-Hungary, Austria-Hungary/Italy, and Germany/Italy can be said to be highly aligned, and even in these cases there are time periods for all three when they are not highly aligned. For instance, Germany/Austria-Hungary is less aligned in the period of negotiations for the Three Emperors' League and in the later 1880s in disputes over the Balkans. For Austria-Hungary/Italy and Germany/Italy, the 1870s are a period of less alignment followed, in the 1880s, by greater alignment. Though Germany/Britain and Germany/Rus-

TABLE 6.7   Findings of Paired Comparisons for 11 Time Periods:
Alignment and Symmetry (Cooperation/Conflict Level)*

	Symmetry of Cooperation		Symmetry of Conflict	
1870-Conclusion of Three Emperors' League (1+2)	60		20	
1870-Conclusion of War-in-Sight Crisis (1+2+3)	59		38	
1870-Outbreak of Russo-Turkish War (1+2+2+4)	58		24	
Turkish Reforms (1875)-Issuing Cong. Berlin Invitations (4+5)	49		10	
Cong. Berlin-Signing of Dual Alliance (6)	64		33	
Attraction of Russia to Dual Alliance-Signing of Three Emperors' Alliance (7)	33		-	
Cong. Berlin-Signing Triple Alliance & British Occupation of Egypt (6+7+8)	45		25	
Cong. Berlin-fall Ferry Gov., end French/German Entente (6+7+8+9)	49		41	
Bulgarian Uprising-Signing 2nd Mediterranean Agr. (10+11+12)	45		27	
End Bulgarian Uprising, French/Italian War Scare-End of 1890 (13+14+15)	43		11	
Bulgarian Uprising-1980 (10+11+12+13+14+15)	29		18	
Percentage of time periods that confirm the Cooperation/Conflict Level (Alignment) Hypothesis	1/11	9%	7/10	70%
Percentage of time periods that confirm the opposite of the Cooperation/Conflict Level (Alignment) Hypothesis	0/11	0%	0/10	0%

*Below 30% is regarded as significant and confirms the Alignment Hypothesis; above 70% is also significant and confirms the opposite of the Alignment Hypothesis.

TABLE 6.8 Individual Dyad Comparisons of the Alignment Hypothesis

Each cell reports, for the comparison of the two dyads, the Symmetry of Cooperation and the Symmetry of Conflict. Values are given as: cooperation % , conflict % / cooperation number , conflict number.

(first dyad)	Ger/Rus	Ger/Frn	Ger/Aus	Ger/Itl	Brt/Rus	Brt/Frn	Brt/Aus	Brt/Itl	Rus/Frn	Rus/Aus	Rus/Itl	Frn/Aus	Frn/Itl	Aus/Itl
Ger/Brt	64 90 / 11 10	43 88 / 7 8	18 50 / 11 6	80 50 / 5 4	22 100 / 9 9	22 80 / 9 5	63 100 / 8 2	80 80 / 5 5	57 100 / 7 6	20 67 / 10 9	·	50 100 / 4 3	0 100 / 3 4	43 80 / 7 5
Ger/Rus		17 100 / 6 8	73 50 / 11 6	100 50 / 5 4	22 78 / 9 9	67 40 / 9 5	63 100 / 8 2	80 40 / 5 3	86 100 / 7 5	60 56 / 10 9	·	100 3 / 4 3	100 100 / 4 3	67 80 / 6 5
Ger/Frn			11 100 / 6 8	50 50 / 4 4	9 9 / 7 8	14 25 / 9 5	17 100 / 6 2	75 33 / 5 3	17 100 / 7 5	10 75 / 7 8	·	25 67 / 4 3	0 3 / 3 4	6 25 / 17 6
Ger/Aus				40 100 / 4 4	71 38 / 7 8	45 60 / 9 5	33 100 / 6 2	40 80 / 6 5	6 67 / 4 3	43 75 / 7 8	·	25 0 / 4 1	33 4 / 3 3	57 6 / 6 4
Ger/Itl					33 100 / 9 9	9 5 / 9 5	6 2 / 6 2	5 25 / 5 4	71 3 / 7 7	50 50 / 10 5	·	100 100 / 1 1	0 3 / 3 3	7 5 / 100 5
Brt/Rus						40 50 / 5 4	73 100 / 9 9	80 75 / 9 8	75 100 / 7 3	10 5 / 25 75	·	50 67 / 4 3	75 3 / 3 3	60 25 / 5 8
Brt/Frn							4 4 / 6 2	5 25 / 5 4	4 75 / 2 2	25 38 / 4 8	·	50 100 / 4 1	3 3 / 3 3	17 6 / 6 4
Brt/Aus								60 75 / 4 4	17 75 / 6 4	8 8 / 4 4	·	67 3 / 3 1	100 3 / 3 3	43 80 / 8 5
Brt/Itl									40 0 / 5 2	38 0 / 8 4	·	0 100 / 1 1	0 2 / 3 4	80 0 / 5 2
Rus/Frn										29 100 / 8 4	·	75 0 / 1 2	100 2 / 2 4	5 33 / 2 3
Rus/Aus											·	4 33 / 2 3	100 2 / 2 4	40 5 / 3 0
Rus/Itl												·	·	17 6 / 0 3
Frn/Aus													67 33 / 3 3	33 6 / 100 4
Frn/Itl														67 0 / 3 1
Aus/Itl														0 100 / 1 4

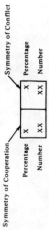

Symmetry of Cooperation

Percentage	X
Number	XX

Symmetry of Conflict

	Percentage	X
	Number	XX

Abbreviations: Ger=Germany; Brt=Great Britain; Rus=Russia; Frn=France; Aus=Austria-Hungary; Itl=Italy.

sia are also highly aligned, their periods of relative nonalignment are more numerous than Austria-Hungary/Italy, Germany/Austria-Hungary, or Germany/Italy, or the alignment ranks are not as high.

After these relatively aligned dyads come Britain/France, Russia/France, Britain/Austria-Hungary, Germany/Italy, Britain/Italy, and France/Austria-Hungary. Once past this group of dyads, we find dyads with relatively few aligned periods. For example, the dyad reveals that Russia/Austria-Hungary displays early intense alignment as early as the Congress of Berlin. Though Russia/Austria-Hungary's rank fluctuates, by the period of the Uprising in Bulgaria to the signing of the Mediterranean agreement, the Russia/Austria-Hungary ranking indicates an unaligned dyad. The remaining dyads, Germany/France, Britain/Russia, France/Italy, and Russia/Italy, display consistently unaligned measurements.

When we compare our relatively aligned and unaligned dyads with the allied and independent ones, we find that the two sets of dyads are largely comparable. But the greater behavioral sensitivity of alignment reveals some important distinctions and suggests why the Alignment Hypothesis is confirmed with the symmetry of conflict. Germany/Austria-Hungary is a good comparative case with alliance and alignment. When we compare Germany/Austria-Hungary with both aligned and unaligned dyads, Austria-Hungary/Italy, Germany/France, Britain/Russia, France/Italy, or Russia/Austria-Hungary, they all confirm the Alignment Hypothesis with conflict symmetry. Yet in Chapter Five, we found Germany/Austria-Hungary an exception to the Alliance Hypothesis. Part of the improvement can be attributed to the lower alignment ranking of Germany/Austria-Hungary in the last periods. The conflict over the Balkans between the two affects their cooperation/Conflict levels. On the alliance ranking, Germany/Austria-Hungary remains the most allied dyad. As a result, with alignment the higher symmetry of conflict for Germany/Austria-Hungary confirms the Alignment Hypothesis dyads, while with alliance the higher symmetries count against confirmation.

The greater behavioral sensitivity also influences the results of Germany/Britain. On the alignment ranking, Germany/Britain becomes relatively more aligned, beginning toward the end of the 1870s and continuing to the French-German détente. Germany/Britain, which has relatively low symmetry of conflict rankings, compares well with most other dyads on alignment. On alliance, however, this is not the case. Throughout the period just discussed Germany/Britain is defined as an independent dyad, and the low symmetry of conflict rankings results in mixed comparisons with Germany/Britain. Indeed, Austria-Hungary/Italy, Germany/Russia, and Germany/Italy, in comparisons with similar aligned and unaligned dyads such as Germany/ France, Britain/Russia, and France/Italy, all significantly confirm the Alignment Hypothesis on symmetry of conflict.

Other contrasts between alliance and alignment are also noticeable, though less effective in confirming our dyads. Russia/ France is unallied throughout the entire twenty-one years. The alignment ranking once again provides us with variation that alliance cannot. Russia/France becomes more aligned in the period after the Three Emperors' League and through about 1880. This alignment ranking change is helpful, though Russia/ France's low symmetry of conflict is too low for a dyad in the middle of the alignment ranking. This result is a reminder to be careful not to place too much emphasis on the sensitivity of our alignment indicator alone. Our confirmations are pairwise comparisons of alignment and behavior. In the Russia/France case, for instance, the greater variability of alignment does not make up for the lowest-ranked symmetry of conflict. While the variability of alignment means Russia/France will now compare well with an aligned dyad such as France/Italy, it will not compare well with aligned dyads Germany/Austria-Hungary or Austria-Hungary/Italy.

Russia/Austria-Hungary is another case where alignment sensitivity cannot overcome unusual symmetry rankings. For instance, in comparison with France/Italy, a very much unaligned state, Russia/Austria-Hungary does not compare well because its symmetry of conflict is ranked so highly. As with Britain/

Russia, another unaligned dyad, the symmetry of conflict of Russia/Austria-Hungary is so high that the comparison is not strongly confirmed with this unaligned dyad. Even Germany/ Austria-Hungary has too low a symmetry of conflict level toward the end of the 1880s for a still relatively unaligned dyad.

Though exceptions to the Alignment Hypothesis exist, the number and strength of dyadic confirmations differ significantly from the previous structural hypotheses. In particular, the greater sensitivity to shifts in cooperation and conflict of alignment contrast with the formal alliance differences.

The alignment finding suggests that the patterns of conflict interaction, at least in this period, are more related to the immediate situations, events, and commitments than to the permanent structural characteristics of the international system. Indeed, all the findings of this chapter—alignment, "alliance use," colonial disputes—encourage us to focus on diplomatic activity and structural attributes which are closely related to the patterns of diplomatic interaction. Moreover, these results should not only be seen in the historical period we have been examining. Their influence should also be viewed from both a contemporary and policy-making perspective. It is with these twin concerns in mind that we conclude our study of the logic of diplomacy.

NOTES

1. The systemic mean was used as the basis for determining high and low symmetry. In several instances we found that distinguishing the category for certain dyads was not clear. Those instances occur widely over time and by dyads.

2. For power and status inconsistency the ranks were split into two equal groups. For alliance, we divided alliance from independence by the presence or absence of alliance months.

3. We use terms such as associative or dissociative to distinguish general cooperative and conflictual patterns of symmetry; from more specific cooperative and conflictual acts.

4. These contrasting patterns of alliance in the data appear to confirm hypotheses suggested at various times by historians. See particularly Schroeder (1976).

5. Yet the independent category as described by the Alliance Hypothesis is highly undifferentiated: given our calculations of dependence/independence, no distinctions were drawn between our independent dyads. We shall try to correct this alliance limitation by expanding the definition of alliance.

6. Some analyses (Taylor, 1954; Rosecrance, 1963) have argued that colonial issues acted as a "safety valve" for tensions in the European system. However, if unequal power dyads are more likely to be related to associative patterns of interaction, then colonial tensions did not act as the "safety valve" for the European system, as has been suggested.

7. In the original analysis (see Alexandroff, 1979), in fact, we chose several other tests of alignment besides the one reported here. The other definitions of alignment included a frequency-of-interaction measure of alignment and a structural-balance measure of alignment. Neither alternative operationalization proved consistently significant but the reader may wish to refer to these measures of alignment as well.

8. Our structural indicator no longer requires division by years. With power attributes, especially, our time divisions had to correspond to years because power was measured annually. Without this restriction we can divide our periods by more natural politically salient events. These divisions also help to distinguish significant shifts in relationships among the powers. The divisions chosen include: (1) 1870 to the conclusion of the Three Emperors' League; (2) 1870 to the conclusion of the War-in-Sight Crisis; (3) 1870 to the outbreak of the Russo-Turkish War; (4) Turkish reforms to the sending of invitations for the Congress of Berlin; (5) the Congress of Berlin to the signing of the Dual Alliance; (6) the attraction of Russia to Dual Alliance to the signing of the Three Emperors'; (7) the Congress of Berlin to the signing of the Triple Alliance and the British occupation of Egypt; (8) the Congress of Berlin to the Ferry government fall and the end of French/German entente; (9) the uprising in Bulgaria to the signing of the Second Mediterranean Agreement; (10) the end of the Bulgarian uprising and the French/Italian war scare to the end of 1890; (11) the uprising in Bulgaria to 1890.

Chapter 7

CONCLUSIONS

The Balance of Diplomacy

Serious debates of the academic and policy-making world have served as a logic of development for this analysis. We have discussed some of those issues earlier in arguments over method and focus. In some ways, the starting point of this study draws its energy from the great American diplomatic historian, 'William Langer. Much of his work on European as well as American international relations was deeply conditioned by the conventions of traditional diplomatic history. Yet Langer (1950: vii-viii) was well aware of the needs and new directions required of international relations.

> The study of diplomacy, if it is to lead to anything worthwhile, must go beyond the mere digest or analysis of documents and negotiations. It must study the fundamental forces and the broad currents that influenced the relations of states to each other.

This analysis has been dedicated to that task, not only from the perspective of the historian but also from the point of view of the political scientist. For the political scientist of international relations, a major unresolved debate concerns the focus of explanation. Should analysis place emphasis on the structures and attributes of the system and its actors or on the behavior and interaction of these parties? The analysis here begins with behavior. Yet while this view takes direction from the historical approach, it also contradicts it. Like the historical approach, this study focuses on the diplomatic activities of the Great Powers to explain the outcomes of international politics. But it contradicts the historical view by arguing that this interaction is not without pattern—there is a logic which defines the activity of these powers. The data of the Situational Analysis Project provided the means to test for that underlying logic. We began with the concept of symmetry in behavior and suggested through the Symmetry Hypothesis that if country A were cooperative toward country B, then country B would be cooperative toward country A. Similarly, if country A were conflictual towards country B, then country B would be conflictual toward country A. Our tests of all the powers for the entire two decades revealed that the pattern of symmetry was strongly confirmed for cooperation and less strongly confirmed for conflict. Since cooperative actions dominated the dimplomatic scene, as the analysis showed, the results confirmed the importance of symmetry in Great Power interaction. Here, then, was the fundamental test of diplomacy and its influence on interstate behavior. For us it was the starting point of explanation.

The examination revealed that symmetry was not the sole pattern of interaction. Conflict, particularly, displayed patterns of asymmetry. The study of the influence process has primarily concerned itself with the nature of conflictual and cooperative outcomes. Whether deterrence (asymmetry) or a conflict spiral model (symmetry) is more appropriate in describing behavior and its outcomes remains a hotly debated theoretical and empirical issue. Moreover, it is not limited to just an academic debate. Policy makers agonize over strategies of firmness or accommodation in international and domestic politics. For these reasons we felt it important to delve further into the symmetry of conflict for these years. The results of the Symmetry Hypothesis seemed to provide some empirical support for the behavioral deterrence view. The frequency of asymmetry of conflict seemed to suggest that conflict would return cooperation. In an effort to test behavioral deterrence, we reanalyzed the data, introducing categories of more (extreme) conflictual actions or less (warning) conflictual actions. Our statement (the Behavior Deterrence Hypothesis) suggested that deterrence would be supported if we found that more extreme conflict actions led to cooperation more frequently than did less extreme conflict actions. This funding would support the deterrence view that credibility and commitment (firmness) would return cooperation. Our results did not, however, confirm the Behavioral Deterrence Hypothesis. More extreme actions did not return cooperation more frequently than less threatening actions.

This leads to some interesting conclusions. The examinations findings reveal that you cannot argue that deterrence rests on general patterns of diplomatic activity. This is an important finding. Contemporary diplomacy has been strongly influenced by nuclear weapons. This is particularly true for those that possess them, but even for those that do not diplomatic bargaining has been strongly influenced by the strategic-diplomatic logic derived from the nuclear-weapons environment. These findings suggest the limitations of deterrence as a credible strategic cum diplomatic technique. The results here suggest the greater probability of a threat-counterthreat pattern. This interaction pattern is the foundation of the spiral model discussed earlier. These findings do not test actual nuclear bargaining. But they raise sufficient doubts to warrant some rethinking of the deterrence model. Certainly, the consequences of an inappropriate model would be serious indeed. At a minimum, the Behavioral Deterrence findings would suggest that strategic deterrence may stand on a less firm empirical foundation than has been assumed up to now.

This early focus on conflict in the Deterrence Hypothesis raises further debates that fuel the direction of the analysis. Along with the structural versus behavioral arguments there exists a conflict over the focus and character of the international system. One view tending to the structural pole emphasizes the formal character of international politics. In this view greater attention is paid to the determinative character of national capabilities or alliance. Equally there is a focus on the international system as a crisis system, with the emphasis on crisis/conflict behavior and war. The alternative view, not as well articulated in international relations or in its literature, sees the system in more behavioral terms. It focuses on informal mechanisms of influence, including cooperation, and it defines the international system as a mixed system of reinforcement and sanctioning.

In order to give voice both to this wider debate and to the more specific debate on structure and behavior, we performed an analysis of the relationship of structural variables to symmetry of behavior. From our investigation of the literature on international relations, particularly of the quantitative international relations writings, we deserve that structure has provided the key independent variables of explanation. We chose to examine the crucial structural variables of the international relations literature—"power," "status," and "alliance."

For "power," as full a description of the capabilities of status of the late nineteenth century was developed. With power defined, we suggested that differences in power between our actors would be related to the symmetry of interaction. Specifically, the Power Hypothesis argued that the more equal the power between nation-state A and nation-state B, then the higher the symmetry of cooperation and conflict; and the less equal the power (or the greater the differences in power), the lower the symmetry of cooperation and conflict between nation-state A and nation-state B.

Each individual power indicator as well as various indexes of power were tested. All the tests of power failed to confirm a significant relationship between power differences, our structural variable, and symmetry, our behavioral variable. The results of the Power Hypothesis therefore suggest that attribute power does not easily explain the patterns of actor influence. Balance of power explanations (Kaplan, 1957; Rosecrance, 1968; Waltz, 1964, 1978) have assumed that power differences determine international system outcomes. Our findings show that this conclusion is not warranted. The relationship between power and influence cannot be confirmed in these crucial twenty-one years.

The failure of the Power Hypothesis, while serious, led to an examination of differences in status in an effort to explain the variations in symmetry of the powers. In status theory, both joint status and status differences, or inconsistencies, have been hypothesized to explain the outcomes of nation-state interaction.

Status, like power, is subject to numerous definitions. Inconsistency adds a complicating twist defining two status categories—achieved and ascribed status. As with power, this analysis tried to define status in its various forms. Because achieved power represents capability and wealth, we employed our broadest definition of power—the combined power index. This index included military strength plus industrial and resource capabilities. For ascribed power we sought indicators of esteem or prestige—the judgments of the international community.

The first test of status theory focused on the influence of the combined status ranks of the dyads on the variations in symmetry. The analysis, following from status theory, hypothesized that the higher the joint status rank of nation-state A and nation-state B, the higher the symmetry of cooperation and the lower the symmetry of conflict. For this status hypothesis—the Cooperation Hypothesis—we tested our powers with all the indicators of status separately, and then combined.

Besides combined status, status theory attempts to explain behavioral outcomes by the differences or inconsistencies in status ranks among nation-states. To test status inconsistency, we hypothesized that the greater the status inconsistency of nation-state A and nation-state B, the higher the symmetry of conflict and the lower the symmetry of cooperation (Status Inconsistency Hypothesis). Multiple definitions of status inconsistency were tested. For instance, status inconsistency was defined as the difference between achieved and ascribed status, regardless of which was greater. Alternately, status inconsistency was defined as the difference between achieved and ascribed status where greater achievement inconsistency was regarded as more likely to lead to higher symmetries of conflict and lower symmetries of cooperation. Finally, status inconsistency was defined so that not only the magnitude and the type of inconsistency were included in the definition, but also the type of actor. Two types of actors, topdogs and underdogs, were identified. With actor types, consistent-status actors (topdogs or underdogs), according to status theory, were more likely to lead to higher symmetries of cooperation and lower symmetries of conflict. In this investigation of status inconsistency, all types of differences were included in our tests of the Status Inconsistency Hypothesis.

Yet after all these tests of combined status rank and status inconsistency, our findings repeated our tests of power. Both the Cooperation Hypothesis and the Status Inconsistency Hypothesis failed to confirm the hypothesized relationship of status to diplomatic activity. Once again, our findings show that the structural-attributes approach—status in this case—does not explain the influence process—the patterns of diplomacy.

Alliance remained the last significant structural approach untested. Of all the approaches, it was the one hypothesized most likely to prove significant in seeking to explain the variation in diplomatic interaction—symmetry. Alliance, like power, was a mechanism of the balance of power. Alliances in these twenty-one years were tools frequently employed in the complex diplomatic activity of the period. Moreover, alliance had overall a political character not seen in our previous attribute examples.

The analysis presumed that the cost of alliances between actors would influence the diplomatic interactions. Therefore, the Alliance Hypothesis argued that the more allied nation-state

A and B, the lower the symmetry of cooperation and conflict, while the less allied (the more independent) nation-state A and B, the higher the symmetry of cooperation and conflict. With the numerous alliances of the Bismarckian Concert the analysis tested this Alliance Hypothesis.

But as with power and with status before it, the test of alliance failed to confirm our Alliance Hypothesis. We were not able to show that the more allied the dyad, the lower the symmetries of interaction. Indeed, an examination of selected dyads revealed that both allied dyads such as Germany/Austria-Hungary and unallied or independent dyads such as Germany/France revealed high symmetries of cooperation. Though the alliance characteristics differed widely, both dyads revealed similar levels of cooperative symmetry. This "paradox of cooperation" underlined the disconfirmation of the Alliance Hypothesis with cooperation, but provided no answer to the relationship of alliance to symmetry. Again, the analysis was left incapable of systematically showing a relationship between our structural attribute and symmetry.

The general tests of all these major structural approaches failed to explain the patterns of symmetry: all three major international relations approaches were disconfirmed. These findings seriously undermined structural explanations of international system outcomes. The structural characteristics identified here do not appear consistently sensitive enough to explain actor interaction with our hypotheses even with just the ranked and therefore relatively crude variations in the symmetry of interaction of all the powers.

Using the "discrete analysis" technique we were capable of moving beyond the general findings. In an effort to explore the failure of structural explanations and to reconstruct the relationship of attribute variables, the analysis turned to a more simple and static categorization of our concepts. For each of our original hypotheses, we defined one associative (cooperative) pattern and one dissociative (conflictual) pattern. For alliance and power, the associative pattern defined was the low symmetry of cooperation and the low symmetry of conflict.

Thus, allied dyads and unequal power dyads were hypothesized to exhibit the dissociative patterns—high conflict symmetry and high cooperation symmetry. The status hypotheses identified associative and dissociative patterns. In these hypotheses, the associative patterns defined was high cooperation symmetry, low conflict symmetry, while the dissociative pattern was low cooperation symmetry, high conflict symmetry. For our status hypotheses, high joint-status dyads or status-consistent dyads were hypothesized to exhibit the associative patterns and low joint-status dyads or status-inconsistent dyads were hypothesized to display dissociative behavior patterns.

From the categorization of all our dyads by behavior types, it became clear that our dyads, defined across all the structural dimensions—power, alliance, and status—failed to display consistently one associative or dissociative pattern. Thus, allied dyads revealed not only patterns of low cooperative symmetry and low conflict symmetry but also patterns of high cooperative symmetry and low conflict symmetry. Independent dyads revealed not only patterns of high cooperation symmetry and high conflict symmetry but also low cooperation symmetry and high conflict symmetry. Power and status differentiations revealed these same mixed patterns.

The European powers reveal dual associative and dissociative patterns of interaction; our hypotheses define single patterns only. This finding helps to clarify our "paradox of cooperation." We found in our alliance analysis that Germany/Austria-Hungary, a highly allied dyad, and Germany/France, an independent dyad, both exhibited highly ranked cooperative symmetry levels. The dual associative patterns, however, solve this paradox. Germany/Austria-Hungary, rather than displaying low cooperation and low conflict, exhibits high cooperation and low conflict. Both patterns are associative, though only one pattern completely supports the Alliance Hypothesis.

While these dual categorizations help to explain the "paradox of cooperation," they do not explain the failure of the structural hypotheses to confirm conflict symmetry. In fact, our dyads revealed not only dual associative and dissociative patterns with like structural powers but crossed patterns as well. Germany/Austria-Hungary, our allied dyad, largely exhibited the associative pattern—low conflict symmetry and high cooperative symmetry. It exhibited a dissociative pattern—high cooperation, high conflict symmetry. Germany/Austria-Hungary was not the only disconfirming allied case. Germany/Russia, another allied dyad, also revealed a dissociative pattern; and Austria-Hungary/Russia, an allied dyad throughout most of these twenty-one years, displayed no associative patterns at all. Similarly, independent dyads—for instance, Russia/France and Britain/France—revealed associative patterns as well as dissociative ones. These contrary patterns were found not only with alliance but with power and status differences.

The patterns of confirmation and disconfirmation of the discrete analysis provide evidence for the failure of the original hypotheses. Furthermore, they give us the means to extend our analysis and to begin to redefine the structural concepts. Our measurements of alliance took into account various alliance differences but failed to distinguish the way in which alliances were used. Historically, the alliances of this period were put to differing purposes. Some, like the Dual Alliance and the Mediterranean Agreements, focused participants' attentions on presumed common foes. They promoted strenthened ties, usually among the signatories.

However, alliances in this period performed functions not compatible with this view of alliance. Bismarck, in particular, the engineer of most of these agreements, used alliances in other, less traditional, ways. Within the Three Emperors' League and Alliance, for instance, he encouraged to bridge differences between foes Austria-Hungary and Russia. And the German-Austrian and German-Russian agreements were used by Bismarck as much to control allies as support them.

With these distinctions, disconfirming cases become explicable. Classical alliance patterns show associative patterns, but the alliances used to bridge differences or constrain allies show dissociative patterns as well. The dissociative patterns of symmetry of Germany/Austria-Hungary, Germany/Russia, and

Austria-Hungary/Russia appear to be a result of the diplomatic complexities introduced by Bismarck into alliance formation and use.

These alliance uses even help to suggest reasons for various independent patterns. In particular, the associative patterns of Russia/France appear to be a reaction to German attempts to isolate France and Russia's sense of growing estrangement from Germany. The numerous agreements pointed against these two states seem to have encouraged cooperative diplomatic inter- actions.

The findings here reveal the complexity of alliances: simple categorizations of alliance appear insufficient. A measure of the number of alliances or number of partners cannot serve to tap the real complexity of alliance functions in the international system. Thus, crude examinations of alliances, such as Singer and Small's (1968), were bound to produce the limited findings they in fact did produce. These authors suggested their findings were a result of the lengthy time period. Our findings argue that it was insufficient attention to the complexity of alliances. The Alliance Hypothesis was disconfirmed, but our analysis has revealed added dimensions which help reveal the more complex relationship between alliances and diplomacy. Indeed, Bis- marck's various alliance uses in this period focus our attention on the diplomatic activities of the alliances and not the alliances themselves. Simple alliance differences do not explain the pat- terns of actor influence.

Further analysis revealed additional explanations for our dis- confirmations with structural characteristics. The interaction of various patterns of structure—alliance, power, and status—may have influenced the contrary patterns. And with power, many of our disconfirmations were states locked in colonial disputes. These conclusions are not generally applicable. They do not describe a consistent relationship between the structural charac- teristics and diplomatic activity. Indeed, our examination of status emphasized the limited extent to which this approach explained the patterns of symmetry at all. Nonetheless, this analysis further added to our understanding of the findings revealed in our initial examination.

The importance of diplomatic uses of alliance in this extended analysis alerted us again to the restricted definition of alliance in the Alliance Hypothesis. Only formal alliances patterns had been employed in our alliance test; the "discrete analysis" suggested the need to broaden the alliance definition. In our final structural test, therefore, we turned to an examination of the relationship between alliance—but now informal alliances—alignment and the patterns of influence. Alignment was defined in behavioral and not legal terms. While a structural characteristic, alignment was neither as formal nor as broadly committing as alliance. Alignment in this analysis was defined as the level of cooperative/conflictual behavior of the dyads. The Alignment Hypothesis was constructed in the same way as previous hypotheses. But in this test, we found a consistent relationship between our new variable and diplomatic patterns. We established that the more aligned nation-state A and nation-state B, the lower the symmetry of conflict; the less aligned nation-state A and nation-state B, the higher the symmetry of conflict. This finding also means that it is not the formal alliance patterns but the informal, diplomatic patterns which identify the influence of structural differences on diplomatic activity.

Indeed, the findings throughout this analysis are consistent. They continually reinforce the picture of a less structured, more mixed international system. Early in the analysis it was observed that conflict was more frequently ignored then cooperation (the No Response Hypothesis), centering attention on the informal modes, of diplomatic behavior. Certainly the structural hypotheses have been found consistently wanting. There is no direct explanation from structural characteristics to the patterns of influence interaction. Instead, it is the "structural-behavioral," "alliance-use," and alignment characteristics linked to the diplomatic actions themselves which explain the patterns of symmetry.

The task of explaining behavior—the logic of diplomacy—is not complete. There are additional dynamic processes to examine. There is a need to examine the interactive quality of structural and "structural-behavior" variables. But this analysis has identified some basic approaches. It has focused our attention on interaction, it has revealed the importance of structural characteristics very closely linked with diplomatic objectives—"structural-behavioral" variables. It has sketched a view of international relations which is more behavioral and more accommodating to cooperative and not just to conflictual actions, as well as to the informal methods of influence.

This view of international politics is valuable not simply for analysts of international relations but to policy makers as well. Our conclusions, for instance, lend an understanding of the diplomatic mechanisms of the Bismarckian Concert, the period we have formally examined. They reveal some of the means by which this period contained serious disruptions. Table 7.1 shows the ranks for all the dyads for all twenty-one years, in respect of alliance, alignment, and, finally, symmetry. Focusing on conflict symmetry[1] and these two structural characteristics, one finds some important contrasts. For instance, too great a fixation on alliances and alliance balance in this period would suggest a split international system. In one camp would be Bismarck's Germany and closely knit to it, Austria-Hungary and Italy. Ties to Russia and Britain directly or indirectly would be drawn. In the other camp the French and the Russian would reside, with the Russians still linked to Germany. The isolation of the French and Germany's close ties to Austria-Hungary would be the governing balance.

Alignment alters this picture. The close German/Austrian rapprochement would be less pronounced; the links of Germany to Austria-Hungary and Russia would be less evident. The stark quality of the alliance picture would be less apparent with this more sensitive diplomatic mechanism.

Conflict symmetry—the patterns of diplomatic activity—reveals the even more subtle diplomatic distance of friends and foes alike. Here Germany/Austria-Hungary exhibits a far less

TABLE 7.1 Twenty-One-Year Comparison: Alliance,
Alignment, Conflict Symmetry

		Alliance	Alignment		Symmetry of	
		Total			Conflict	
		Alliance		Level of*		
Dyad	Rank	Months	Rank	Coop/Con	Rank	%
Germany/Aus-Hun	1	1047	2	54.90	6	52
Germany/Italy	2	438.5	3	54.32	3	40
Aus-Hun/Italy	3	405.5	1	55.50	3	30
Germany/Russia	4	231	6	52.05	5	46
Russia/Aus-Hun	5	213	12	49.44	9	61
Britain/Italy	6	87	7	51.96	2	25
Britain/Aus-Hun	7	82.5	5	52.81	-	-
Germany/Britain	8	46.5	8	51.62	8	55
Britain/Russia	9	0	11	50.52	11	72
France/Russia	9	0	4	53.23	1	0
France/Aus-Hun	9	0	9	51.34	-	-
Britain/France	9	0	10	50.64	7	53
France/Germany	9	0	13	47.31	10	69
Italy/Russia	9	0	14	43.18	-	-
France/Italy	9	0	15	42.78	12	100

*Systemic Average of Level of Cooperation/Conflict for the twenty-one years is 51.45.

associative pattern than alliance would have revealed. Russia/
Austria-Hungary and Germany/Russia are at greater distances
also. Britain/Italy, on the other hand, is more associative than
when described with alliance. Britain/France is more associative
than either alliance or alignment would suggest. The balancing
of friends and adversaries is more evident; the divisions are less
stark with the patterns of diplomatic interactions. Commitments aside, Germany remained less associative to Austria-Hungary than the alliance agreements revealed. Other patterns of
symmetry also contrasted with the international system por-
trayed with alliances. The true balancing role of Bismarck and
others is reflected not in power or alliance but in behavioral or
diplomatic terms. Focusing on this "balance of diplomacy"
rather than the more structural divisions suggests that the weakness of the Bismarckian period was only that the balancing
could not be carried far enough. Bismarck was successful in

maintaining relative stability in the system, but he could or did not bridge many of the conflicts. Russia/Austria-Hungary, already in the Bismarckian years, maintained a higher symmetry of conflict, and France/Russia exhibited a rather too strong pattern of association. What follows after 1890 reflects those Bismarckian conditions rather than the complete overthrow of the Bismarkian system.

This balance of diplomacy, the balancing of adversaries and friends, is not simply a recipe for multipolarity, though the two are not unrelated. The former focuses on diplomatic activity—the informal mechanisms—while multipolarity directs attention to formal mechanisms. And as we've tried to show (Table 7.1) there can be distinct and differing, though related, pictures of the international sytem, depending on which variables one chooses to focus on. Also, we do not wish to consign our analysis to strictly a historical Bismarckian environment. Indeed, the informal mechanisms, the picture of the mixed international system described in this analysis, may not only be academically interesting but a vital means to maintain the stability of contemporary international politics.

There has been a struggle, particularly in recent American foreign policy, to adjust American actions to the "new realities" of international relations. At the same time, there have been many voices demanding the reassertion of American power and leadership, fearing that the United States has weakened its international position, particularly vis-à-vis the Soviet Union. The debate over American foreign policy does take positions that contrast more formal structural interpretations of international politics with more informal ones. The former view relies on power and on the enhancement of old ties and alliances, while the latter appears to stress diplomatic interaction and informal mechanisms of adjustment.

The emergence of the mixed system can be pinpointed with the change in behavior toward the People's Republic of China during the Nixon Administration. As part of a larger strategy of détente, President Nixon and Henry Kissinger initiated diplomatic policies that broke with American Cold War Strategy. The debate over the appropriate American diplomatic strategy that has ensued since raises the kinds of questions that this study has tried to investigate in a more formal way. It provides us with some scope to comment, then, on the recent arguments over appropriate American foreign policy directions.

What has struck contemporary observers of American foreign policy as ironic is that the administration responsible for the initial moves toward a revised "mixed diplomacy" was one which hoped to reestablish American dominance (even in the earlier Cold War sense) in the international system but without the cost that older strategies had imposed, Vietnam being the most glaring cost. The strategy of the Nixon Administration was to stabilize relations with its principal adversary—the Soviet Union—and reduce the cost of containment. The triangular relationship—between Russia, China, and the United States—was designed to promote stability without the accompanying burden to the American government and its people.

This new triangular strategy, particularly the element of the so-called "China card," seemed intended to balance adversaries, whatever the ideological cleavages. The greater part of the subsequent debate has revolved around how far the United States should go in drawing China close to the United States. Certainly the Carter Administration veered from an early policy of even-handedness, trying to deal with the Communist adversaries in almost separate bilateral terms. From the summer of 1978, the United States favored China in terms of technology transfer and, of course, in the normalization of relations with China on January 1, 1979.

Part of the difficulty of assessing the value of the triangular relationship (and by inference the mixed diplomatic style) has been the competing objectives of the strategy itself. Though both Kissinger and Nixon denied any plan to use China in an effort to "soften up" the Soviets, to encourage a more cooperative stance toward American initiatives, it is clear that the triangular relationship was a fillip to their central concern, United States-Soviet relations. And it has been pointed out (Garrett, 1979: 251) that the relationship is not a symmetric one. Of the three actors, the United States has been in the most favorable position because of the depth of animosity in the Sino-Soviet split. Even during cool or poor relations between the United States and either the Soviet Union or China, U.S. relations with these two individually have been better than relations between the Soviet Union and China. Furthermore, it is evident that there continue to be only two superpowers, not three. And indeed, arguments have been put forward which suggest that a triangular relationship is meaningless because the world remains one defined by the power of the United States and the Soviet Union. Thus, using the "China card" cannot alter the power equation and may indeed cause a stiff Russian reaction, because of what might be perceived from the Sovied perspective as an American effort to encircle the Soviet Union.

Responding first to the last point, the analysis here suggests that viewing the strategy along power lines misses the logic of the "balance of diplomacy". It is not that China primarily affects the power equation, because there is no direct linkage of power and interaction, as we have established here. Instead, the triangular relationship affects the influence level; the balancing improves the chances of maintaining stability. If anything, the analysis argues that the "China card" had been too narrowly conceived by the recent policy makers. The United States should have encouraged more effective relationships between China and Western Europe and China and Japan. But the détente strategy failed to see the wider "balance of diplomacy" logic. Furthermore, because the balance of diplomacy is not a structural balance logic where the enemy of my enemy is my friend, it suggests that the United States should encourage the Chinese leadership to seek some modicum of understanding with the Soviet Union. The polarization or asymmetry, if too serious, is likely to undermine the effectiveness of a mixed strategy. It was evident that the Sino-Vietnam conflict, which was strongly influenced by Sino-Russian relations, did not re-dound to American advantage. A serious mixed negotiating style must focus on the balance of symmetries, both conflict and cooperation, among all the major actors.

The importance of the balance of diplomacy is not only apparent in the superpower or near superpower arena; it is relevant to regional systems. Certainly from the Nixon Administration on, the United States has tried to stabilize the Middle East. In particular, it has tried to achieve a settlement of the Arab-Israeli conflict. In doing so, it has sought to win friends in the Arab world, avoiding the near isolation that has dominated American policy there since 1967. From the perspectives of the Nixon and Ford Administrations this initiative was required to prevent Soviet domination, given Arab anger over American support for Israel. Increasingly during the Carter Administration, the security of oil supply to the West has dominated American Middle East concerns and forged a consensus in the Carter Administration to find a solution to the conflict.

In the Middle East, as in the superpower relationship, diplomatic activity has moved American policy away from an earlier more rigid and formal pattern. The break in the pattern of American policy emerged from the violence of the 1973 conflict between Israel and its neighbors. In what has become one of contemporary diplomacy's most skillful episodes, Henry Kissinger manipulated the crisis to restrict Soviet influence, save Egypt's trapped Third Army—and its honor and capacity to bargain—and begin a negotiating process that led to two Egyptian-Israeli agreements and a Syrian-Israeli agreement. Shuttle diplomacy's real triumph was to break the American isolation and extend American influence into the Arab world, with not only Egypt but Syria, yet without the loss of Israeli confidence. As Steven Spiegel (1979: 345) has argued, Kissinger "attempted to establish a momentum that would create a new diplomatic direction while the U.S. remained at the center of the process."

The shuttle diplomacy momentum of Kissinger diplomacy ran its course. With the advent of the Carter Administration there was a new American effort to seek a comprehensive settlement. An incremental strategy was abandoned. Partly because Carter's policy was not initially as critically defined by the Soviet issue, early administration moves included diplomatic activities to include the Russians. The Carter Administration

attempted to reconvene the Geneva Conference, and prepara-
tory to that the United States and the Soviet Union issued a
joint communique on October 1, 1977 in which the United
States used for the first time the phrase, "legitimate rights of
the Palestinians."

This more encompassing approach was blocked by a most
unlikely source—Egypt's Anwar Sadat. Sadat's decision to go to
Israel forced the United States, after some hesitation, to fall in
line with a much narrower Egyptian-Israeli and then Egyptian-
Israeli-American framework. The final fruits of that effort have
been the much heralded Camp David Accords. These accords
remained committed to the original American purpose of com-
prehensiveness, yet in practice they amounted to bilateral accords which could not be expanded initially to include other
parties. The second, however, framed a comprehensive settlement, premised on the resolution of the Palestinian problem.

If Camp David was perceived by American decision makers as
a step to an overall settlement of the Arab-Israeli conflict (and
it is not clear that it was), it certainly has not proven to be such
a step. Indeed, Camp David has taken the most positive balancing element—Egypt—and so polarized its relations with the
rest of the Arab world that Egypt is no longer an effective
bridge to other Arab elements in the Middle East. The accord
has acted to separate, to restrict American action, not to open
up balance of diplomacy possibilities. In part, this result derives
from a continuing American policy which divides the Arab
world into radical and moderate elements. Egypt under Sadat
has been regarded as a moderate element in the Arab equation.
From the American perspective, Sadat formed the core of a
diplomatic strategy to draw moderate Arab states—Jordan, Ku-
wait, Saudi Arabia—into a wider Israeli settlement but freeze
out radicals: Iraq, Libya, even possibly Syria. While the strategy
on the surface sought a more mixed system of diplomacy
including Arab and Israeli states, it never saw the possibilities of
a wider Arab strategy. The consequences have been that Egypt
is now isolated from moderates and radicals alike and America
has no capacity to act with key Arab actors, particularly Iraq

and Syria. As recent conflict in the Persian Gulf has revealed, the American capacity to stabilize the region through a balancing of diplomacy is not apparent. The Camp David agreements have produced rigidity, not the needed flexibility, because the United States failed to see the true potential of a more mixed informal diplomatic system.

The potential of the mixed negotiating system and the balance of diplomacy has been more illusory than real in the last ten years of so-called détente. While much debate has accompanied this strategy, concrete actions have not increased the potential for influence, not even the conditions of stability in the international system. The changes have been half-hearted or they have hidden old logics of bipolar dominance behind the facade of a "new diplomacy." These policies have not unleashed the creative potential of diplomacy; they may have unfortunately constrained it.

Indeed, applying the logic of multilateral diplomacy to American foreign policy would call for far more creative actions with the superpowers, the regional powers, and allies as well. It may well be time to rethink some of the limitations of the bipolar strategy in Europe, as well as with Russia or the Middle East. Various ill-timed diplomatic starts have occurred with Europe, most notably the Kissinger policy of the "Year of Europe." But once again, Cold War logic has darkened the glimmerings of a new diplomatic pattern. American policy has urged greater independence for its European allies, but equally it has called on the Europeans to "toe the American line" in situations in the Middle East and elsewhere. A balance of diplomacy strategy would pay less attention to the formal elements of Europe—NATO and the Warsaw Pact. It would seek a greater balance of actions in West and East alike. It would look for avenues of influence beyond the narrow Cold War bounds. The older strategies are strategies of weakness, not strength. The balance of diplomacy, not just for the United States but for Europe as well, is a strategy of confidence that assumes the strength of our Western European allies, particularly at the level of domestic politics. The implementation of a mixed negotiating system suggests confidence in diplomatic strategies rather than formal structural elements of the system. It does not ignore military capacity but integrates it into a broader dynamic model of the international system. Military capacity becomes an element of a much broader flexible diplomatic pattern.

The logic of diplomacy is important not only in a historical or an academic vein. It has serious lessons for contemporary international policy making. To date its potential remains largely untapped. Indeed, the possibilities for a more flexible international politics may have been positively harmed by the false starts of recent Cold War strategies. It is hoped that the theoretic and empirical work done here can galvanize further thinking in these directions, and more work to extend and fill in the logic of diplomacy. Until then, the author's hope remains that diplomacy will not be ignored in world politics. The world does so at its own peril.

NOTE

1. The "paradox of cooperation" and the inability to explain cooperative symmetry variations suggest that cooperation may be used in a formal diplomatic manner: cooperative actions may lead to cooperative responses regardless of other dyadic differences.

APPENDIX A

METHODOLOGY:
MATCHING HYPOTHESES AND TECHNIQUES

Hypotheses are guesses about possible lawful relationships in the real world. Confirmed hypotheses are building blocks of theory whether in the natural or the social sciences. Hypotheses begin with descriptive concepts. In our case such concepts include diplomatic interactions, alliance commitments, status, power, etc. Like all descriptive concepts, ours are found in language and not in the real world. In order to test the proposed relationship between concepts referred to in hypothesis we must identify clear empirical references—the facts of the real world—for those concepts.

For instance, diplomatic interactions, the primary descriptive concept here, has many possible empirical referents. However, in this analysis the facts are the events, the interactions of our powers—Great Britain, France, Germany, Russia, Austria-Hungary, and Italy. Furthermore, the data of the Situational Analysis Project employed here define consistently and systematically the actions of all the powers for these twenty-one years of inquiry. The definitions of this event project provide, in other words, clear empirical referents for the descriptive concept—diplomatic interactions.

Next we must clarify the properties of those facts we wish to name. In diplomatic interactions properties may be physical or verbal, cooperative or conflictual; we may describe our interactions as flexible or obdurate. Here, however, we've decided on the crucial property of symmetry.

Finally, and depending on the hypothesis, the property may be attached to qualitative, comparative, or quantitative descriptive concepts. As a consequence, the properties exemplifying those concepts will be measured somewhat differently and employ different rules of correspondence with the real number system. In our example, once again, our basic descriptive concept is diplomatic interactions and the property symmetry. In this study we wish to examine, at least initially, whether our patterns of interaction for all our powers from 1870 to 1890 exemplify symmetry or not. The descriptive concept is clearly qualitiative, and as a result we will measure our property nominally: an interaction will be either symmetric or asymmetric, not both. Furthermore, we will employ contingent percentages to display whether our patterns of interaction are symmetric or not.

This tying of techniques to statements is all important; the identification of the appropriate measurement and test depends largely on the hypothesis you are stating and not the type of statistical technique you wish to employ in your analysis.

Our test of symmetry was clearly qualitative. When we turn, however, to compare and explain the levels of symmetry, we wish to explain the differences in symmetry and new concepts such as alliance, power, status, and alignment. All these further structural hypotheses contain two descriptive concepts, one structural and the other behavioral. An alliance hypothesis, for example, includes alliance, the independent concept, and dyadic symmetry, the dependent concept. We wish to test a hypothesis which expresses the relationship between dyadic alliance differences and dyadic symmetry differences. The Alliance Hypothesis, like our other structural hypotheses, should express a relationship which accounts for greater or lesser symmetry levels of interaction. Thus, the hypothesis is no longer concerned with the mere existence of symmetry, as in the first hypothesis; instead, we are interested in testing whether more or less alliance is related consistently to more symmetry, less symmetry, or equal symmetry among comparisons of pairs of our powers. All these relations are comparative in nature and no longer just qualitative; our properties of alliance and symmetry should be measured ordinally in order to test whether more alliance between one dyad and another leads to more symmetry or less symmetry.

To test this explicit comparative hypothesis we need to measure alliance and symmetry differences comparatively. The symmetry differences are, in fact, measured by a restricted ratio scale from 0 to 100 percent. However, our hypothesis is comparative. Therefore, we will employ an ordinal rank measurement. If our hypothesis had defined a difference equation relationship, we would have used the ratio measurements. Our guess about a lawful relationship is, however, only comparative: this is the extent to which we are presently able to understand relationships between our concepts. The most efficient way to accomplish this comparison is to systematically examine our facts by a paired comparison analysis. Thus, we will rank our dyads by alliance and symmetry differences and compare every instance of alliance rank and symmetry rank with every other instance, pairwise, of alliance and symmetry.

An example of such a paired comparison is provided below. The sample test (Table A.1) displays the ranking of five dyads or five pairs of states. Testing an alliance hypothesis would yield [N(N-1)1/2] or ten pairwise comparisons of the suggested proposition. We should find in this example of alliance and symmetry that since dyads 1 through 5 are ranked from more independence (less alliance) to less independence, then for our hypothesis to be confirmed for all instances of comparison (100 percent confirmation) our symmetry rank should run from more symmetry to less symmetry (1 to 5). In our example, four out of ten (40 percent) of the comparisons would accord with the hypothesis the more independent two dyads, the more the symmetry of interaction between the two dyads. We would obtain these results by first comparing dyads 1 and 2 and would see that 3-4, the ranks on the dependent variable, accord with the direction hypothesized. Since we need to compare every

TABLE A.1   A Sample Paired-Comparison Ranking

Dyad Number	Independent Indicator Rank–More Independence	Level of Symmetry Rank–More Symmetry
1	1	3
2	2	4
3	3	5
4	4	1
5	5	2

instance, we would next compare dyads 1 and 3 and recognize 3-5 accords with the hypothesis as well. When we come to our next pairwise comparison, dyads 1 and 4, we see the symmetry rankings 3-1 do not correspond with the hypothesis. In this way we would proceed to compare all our dyads and summarize our findings by taking the percentage of cases that correctly correspond to the direction our properties are hypothesized to take.

This method of comparison just described closely parallels that employed by the ordinal measure of association, Kendall's tau without ties. Kendall's tau is described as: tau = $(S_1 - S_2)/(S_1 + S_2)$. S_1 is the number of paired comparisons on which two objects are similarly ordered and S_2 is the number of paired comparisons on which two objects are inversely ordered. $S_1 + 2$ is the total number of comparisons. When two concepts are perfectly associated tau is either $+1$ or -1; when random association prevails tau is 0. We are concerned of course to compare the instances of pairwise agreement with our hypotheses, and therefore, 40 percent in our example is the figure we are interested in. Nevertheless, Kendall's tau provides us with a standard of comparison. According to Kendall's tau, a random association, 0, provides no reduction in error on one variable by knowing the other variable; we would be as likely to guess incorrectly as correctly the orderings of rankings on the variables by knowing one variable. A Kendall's tau of 1 would reduce our error to nothing; we would be able to guess correctly all the orderings of the objects by knowing the comparisons on one variable. In the sample case we just described, we would have reduced the error by 20 percent. Given the sensitivity, complexity, and variability of interstate behavior, a reduction of 40 percent in error in making comparisons would seem to provide a standard for our hypotheses suggesting at a minimum further analysis. Thus, for the paired comparison analyses that follow in this study, levels of 70 percent and 30 percent pairwise agreement for all instances of comparison will be used as a standard of significance.

One additional feature of analysis should be noted. Most of our independent variables are national characteristics—attributes—and therefore not initially dyadic in form; all our rankings for analysis, however, are by dyads. In order to provide comparisons of all the dyads, an ordered metric is employed to provide differences and totals for all sets of dyads. An ordered metric consists of double ranking the atttribute

> Co-operative concepts are so defined that one can rank-order objects or events in a population in terms of the extent to which they exhibit the property named by a concept. With an ordered metric we then also rank-order the magnitudes of the differences between extents to which two objects or events exhibit a property (Kelley, 1978a: 3-23).

In the next example, the four hypothetical states possess 100 percent of some variable divided in the following manner:

Shares of Attribute Divided among Four Actors
(100 percent total)

A	50
B	20
C	16
D	14

If we were next to rank the differences in magnitude, from largest to smallest, for all shares, we would have an ordered

metric and the means to order our dyads. The differences and
the dyadic ranks would be as follows:

TABLE A.2   An Ordered Metric

Differences	Magnitude of Differences	Shares
	A	50
30	–B	20
4	–C	16
2	–D	14

	Rank Differences of Dyads	
	Absolute	Rank Order
A-B	30	3
A-C	34	2
A-D	36	1
B-C	4	5
B-D	6	4
C-D	2	6

In this manner, we provide a means to compare ordinally the
differences between *all* our dyads.

Finally, the paired-comparison analysis additionally—and this
is very important—provides us with a practical method for
longitudinal analysis. Our assumption is that behavior has a
finite degree of influence; while the influence length is unknown, certainly beyond several years, A's particular behavior is
not likely to influence B's responses (this, of course, is somewhat tempered by the intensity and scope of the particular
behavior). An analysis which simply collapsed all twenty-one
years into one paired-comparison analysis—as correlations do—
would be theoretically and practically valueless. Here, however,
in order to capture the limited extent of influence of behavior
and provide a relatively frequent analysis of behavioral interaction among all our dyads, the levels of symmetry are calculated every three years. Thus, we hypothesize that the effects
(or influence) of A's behavior accumulate up to three years in
regard to B's responses. In addition, to capture the continuous

effects of behavior in interstate actions we decided to calculate a running average; in each succeeding three-year calculation a further year's behavior was added, while the earliest year's interactions were removed from the calculations of symmetric behavior calculations for all dyads over the twenty-one years. Here, then, our paired comparisons provided us with a precise comparative time-series analysis of symmetric behavior and various structural variables.

The more conservative nature of the estimating techniques here does not limit in any significant way the complexity of possible hypotheses; our limitations are reflected, as they should be, in the extent of our theoretical knowledge. In practice most analysts ignore this logic. Rather than allowing the hypotheses to dictate the measurements and the appropriate techniques, most employ techniques inappropriate to the hypotheses to be tested. The use of sophisticated statistical techniques largely assumes that the hypothesis expresses the relationship between descriptive concepts in difference terms. Yet almost invariably it is the quantitative technique itself which determines the difference relationship between independent and dependent variables. The techniques employed here consciously attempt to avoid that dilemma. Our assertion here is that the complexity of technique is no guarantee of a closer fit in testing lawful knowledge; indeed, frequently quantitative statistical techniques detract from efforts to explore rigorously international politics. The end results in quantitative international relations have been, too frequently, highly estimated findings of no particular value in explaining international politics. The overriding concern for interval and ratio measurements is therefore excessive and misplaced; whatever measurements and analysis fit the hypothesis in testing relationships should be the ones used, whether nominal, ordinal, or quantitative.

APPENDIX B

TABLES

TABLE B.1   Symmetry Levels by Directed Dyads for all Powers, for all Years

		Total Symmetry	Symmetry of Cooperation	Symmetry of Conflict
Germany to:	(194)*			
Britain	(46)	65%	69%	55%
Russia	(51)	59	64	47
Austria	(53)	80	87	50
France	(29)	69	79	60
Italy	(15)	80	92	0
Britain to:	(169)			
Germany	(56)	63%	66%	56%
Russia	(42)	74	83	63
Austria	(27)	56	56	0
France	(30)	77	76	78
Italy	(14)	64	73	33
Russia to:	(155)			
Germany	(67)	67%	78%	46%
Britain	(40)	83	85	80
Austria	(33)	67	67	67
France	(13)	69	75	0
Italy	(2)	-	-	-
Austria to:	(122)			
Germany	(49)	74%	79%	55%
Britain	(22)	64	67	0
Russia	(24)	75	87	56
France	(4)	-	-	-
Italy	(23)	61	68	25
France to:	(83)			
Germany	(28)	86%	88%	82%
Britain	(22)	64	81	17
Russia	(18)	56	63	0
Austria	(6)	50	60	0
Italy	(9)	100	100	100
Italy to:	(81)			
Germany	(28)	50%	48%	67%
Britain	(13)	69	75	0
Russia	(1)	-	-	-
Austria	(29)	55	57	50
France	(10)	90	75	100

*Number of interactions.

TABLE B.2   Symmetry of Interactions (Total Dyad): Total Symmetry*

Time Period	Total # of Dyads	Ger/Brt	Ger/Rus	Ger/Frn	Ger/Aus	Ger/It	Brt/Rus	Brt/Frn	Brt/Aus	Brt/It	Rus/Frn	Rus/Aus	Frn/Aus	Frn/It	Aus/It
1870-73	7	1 75	4 50	6 56	4 60	—	7 50	3 67	—	—	—	2 71	—	—	—
1873-75	8	5 67	8 25	3 83	—	—	4 75	1 100	—	—	6 63	7 50	—	—	1 100
1874-76	11	8 64	10 43	3 91	4 83	—	6 70	1 100	11 25	—	9 50	5 69	1 100	—	5 80
1875-77	10	8 46	7 47	1 92	3 83	6 67	4 77	—	10 44	10 33	11 45	6 73	1 100	—	3 80
1876-78	11	7 63	8 53	1 100	2 82	—	4 77	5 67	9 47	8 25	11 25	6 64	—	—	—
1877-79	8	5 68	3 76	1 100	4 74	—	2 79	—	6 57	11 25	—	7 56	5 67	5 67	—
1878-80	11	4 71	3 78	1 100	7 60	0	2 79	7 60	6 56	—	—	10 50	—	3 88	9 40
1879-81	10	7 63	4 83	6 67	8 53	10 0	—	5 76	9 71	—	—	1 100	—	2 90	8 47
1880-82	10	7 55	3 86	—	5 69	10 30	—	4 70	9 33	—	—	1 100	—	1 100	7 41
1881-83	8	5 70	3 82	6 63	6 65	8 33	2 78	4 71	—	—	—	1 100	1 100	—	8 50
1882-84	9	9 44	4 71	3 82	5 82	7 60	1 90	4 64	—	—	—	3 75	—	—	—
1883-85	7	6 52	2 89	2 87	5 76	—	1 88	7 50	—	—	—	4 78	—	—	8 50
1884-86	10	7 52	4 67	5 73	3 78	10 43	1 84	8 50	6 60	8 88	—	4 67	—	—	8 65
1885-87	12	7 70	10 61	8 67	3 81	6 62	2 71	11 60	4 76	2 88	12 57	9 63	—	—	10 70
1886-88	13	9 66	12 57	12 50	2 88	5 75	7 —	5 75	4 79	3 89	11 60	13 50	—	—	10 65
1887-89	12	8 68	7 73	—	2 92	4 81	—	5 80	5 80	3 50	11 60	9 67	—	—	10 —
1888-90	9	6 63	9 40	—	1 100	5 73	3 89	5 89	—	8 50	4 86	—	—	—	7 57

SYMMETRY OF COOPERATION

Time Period	Total # of Dyads	Ger/Brt	Ger/Rus	Ger/Frn	Ger/Aus	Ger/It	Brt/Rus	Brt/Frn	Brt/Aus	Brt/It	Rus/Frn	Rus/Aus	Frn/Aus	Frn/It	Aus/It
1870-73	7	1 100	4 67	7 0	6 60	—	—	5 67	—	—	—	—	—	—	—
1873-75	7	—	7 0	—	—	—	—	—	—	—	—	6 50	—	—	1 100
1874-76	11	8 57	8 57	1 100	4 83	6 67	4 83	1 100	11 25	—	—	7 67	1 100	—	6 80
1875-77	10	8 50	7 57	1 100	2 83	—	3 80	—	10 44	11 —	8 56	5 76	1 100	—	3 80
1876-78	11	5 69	8 50	1 100	3 90	6 —	4 81	6 67	9 47	9 —	10 25	6 67	1 100	1 100	—
1877-79	8	5 81	3 83	1 100	2 84	—	4 82	—	7 57	8 —	10 25	6 60	1 100	—	—
1878-80	11	6 79	4 83	1 100	4 83	10 0	3 86	7 60	7 56	10 —	—	9 50	—	10 0	0
1879-81	10	5 75	3 92	1 100	4 77	10 0	—	5 75	8 71	—	—	1 100	—	5 75	9 25

TABLE B.2 (Continued)

Time Period	Total # of Dyads	Ger/Brt	Ger/Rus	Ger/Frn	Ger/Aus	Ger/Itl	Brt/Rus	Brt/Frn	Brt/Aus	Brt/Itl	Rus/Frn	Rus/Aus	Frn/Aus	Frn/Itl	Aus/Itl
1880-82	10	6 55	2 89	7 50	5 80	10 25	– –	4 81	9 33	– –	– –	1 100	– –	3 83	8 47
1881-83	8	6 50	1 100	– –	5 80	8 29	– –	4 86	– –	– –	– –	1 100	– –	1 100	7 43
1882-84	9	9 0	1 100	6 63	2 83	8 50	4 75	3 77	– –	– –	– –	4 75	– –	– –	7 55
1883-85	7	6 20	1 100	3 82	5 75	8 –	2 86	7 0	– –	– –	– –	4 80	– –	– –	– –
1884-86	10	9 43	2 83	3 82	3 82	7 50	1 88	10 0	6 60	4 88	– –	5 80	– –	– –	7 50
1885-87	12	7 76	10 67	5 86	2 94	8 75	3 96	10 67	6 81	4 88	10 67	1 100	– –	– –	9 73
1886-88	11	6 80	11 65	10 67	1 100	5 81	1 100	6 80	4 83	3 89	8 75	– –	– –	– –	9 78
1887-89	9	5 84	10 65	9 67	1 100	5 84	– –	3 86	3 86	2 89	7 75	– –	– –	– –	8 74
1888-90	8	5 79	8 63	– –	1 100	4 80	3 88	3 88	– –	6 67	1 100	– –	– –	– –	6 67

SYMMETRY OF CONFLICT

Time Period	Total # of Dyads	Ger/Brt	Ger/Rus	Ger/Frn	Ger/Aus	Ger/Itl	Brt/Rus	Brt/Frn	Brt/Aus	Brt/Itl	Rus/Frn	Rus/Aus	Frn/Aus	Frn/Itl	Aus/Itl
1870-73	5	2 50	5 0	1 63	– –	– –	4 33	– –	– –	– –	– –	2 50	– –	– –	– –
1873-75	5	2 67	3 50	1 71	– –	– –	4 0	– –	– –	– –	4 0	– –	– –	– –	– –
1874-76	6	3 75	4 67	2 83	– –	– –	5 50	– –	– –	– –	6 0	1 100	– –	– –	– –
1875-77	6	5 33	2 75	1 83	– –	– –	2 75	– –	– –	5 50	6 0	4 60	– –	– –	– –
1876-78	8	6 33	3 67	7 100	7 0	– –	2 73	– –	– –	5 33	7 0	4 57	– –	– –	– –
1877-79	7	7 0	3 67	5 100	5 3	– –	2 77	– –	– –	5 33	7 0	4 50	– –	1 100	– –
1878-80	8	7 0	3 63	– –	5 33	7 –	2 71	– –	– –	– –	– –	4 50	7 0	1 100	– –
1879-81	8	7 0	5 71	1 100	6 33	– 0	– –	– –	– –	– –	– –	1 100	– –	1 100	1 100
1880-82	8	1 –	7 33	1 100	7 33	4 50	– –	6 43	– –	– –	– –	1 100	– –	1 100	4 50
1881-83	8	1 100	6 33	– –	8 25	– 50	1 100	6 43	– –	– –	10 0	1 100	– –	1 100	6 33
1882-84	7	3 80	6 33	– –	3 80	1 100	1 100	5 50	– –	– –	11 0	– –	– –	– –	6 33
1883-85	6	2 82	6 50	– –	3 75	3 –	– –	5 60	– –	– –	10 0	4 67	– –	– –	– –
1884-86	9	4 71	8 33	1 100	3 75	9 0	2 88	6 60	– –	– –	– –	5 67	– –	– –	7 50
1885-87	11	4 50	4 50	2 63	3 60	4 33	2 78	4 50	10 0	– –	10 0	4 50	– –	1 100	9 40
1886-88	11	8 33	6 43	2 67	8 33	8 33	4 50	2 67	11 0	– –	11 0	4 50	– –	1 100	7 40
1887-89	10	8 33	6 43	7 40	– 50	4 50	– –	10 67	10 0	– –	10 0	2 67	– –	1 100	9 25
1888-90	8	3 25	4 14	– –	– –	5 –	1 100	1 100	– –	5 0	5 0	2 67	– –	1 100	5 0

*In each dyad column, the first figure is the rank of the dyad; the second figure is the symmetry percentage. Due to lack of interactions, there is no dyad column for Russia/Italy.

Abbreviations: Ger = Germany; Brt = Great Britain; Frn = France; Aus = Austria-Hungary; Rus = Russia; Itl = Italy.

TABLE B.3 Symmetry of Interactions, Five-Year Breakdown (Total Dyad)

Time Periods	Ger/Brt	Ger/Rus	Ger/Frn	Ger/Aus	Ger/Itl	Brt/Rus	Brt/Frn	Brt/Aus	Brt/Itl	Rus/Frn	Rus/Aus	Rus/Itl	Frn/Aus	Frn/Itl	Aus/Itl
TOTAL SYMMETRY															
1870-74	83 / 1	60 / 5	58 / 7	60 / 5	. / .	50 / 8	75 / 2	. / .	. / .	67 / 4	71 / 3	. / .	. / .	. / .	. / .
1875-79	64 / 8	63 / 9	94 / 1	76 / 6	67 / 7	78 / 5	80 / 2	52 / 11	20 / 13	45 / 12	62 / 10	. / .	80 / 2	0 / 14	80 / 2
1880-84	52 / 10	84 / 3	70 / 6	72 / 5	27 / 12	80 / 4	65 / 8	25 / 13	. / .	67 / 7	92 / 1	. / .	33 / 11	90 / 2	56 / 9
1885-90	68 / 10	53 / 13	76 / 7	83 / 2	72 / 8	80 / 4	79 / 5	79 / 5	81 / 3	71 / 9	60 / 12	. / .	. / .	100 / 1	63 / 11
SYMMETRY OF COOPERATION															
1870-74	100 / 1	75 / 4	50 / 8	60 / 7	. / .	100 / 1	75 / 4	. / .	. / .	67 / 6	80 / 3	. / .	. / .	. / .	. / .
1875-79	74 / 7	61 / 10	100 / 1	84 / 3	67 / 8	83 / 4	80 / 5	52 / 11	0 / 13	50 / 12	64 / 9	. / .	100 / 1	. / .	80 / 5
1880-84	35 / 11	91 / 1	67 / 7	79 / 4	22 / 13	78 / 5	76 / 6	33 / 12	. / .	67 / 7	90 / 2	. / .	50 / 10	83 / 3	58 / 9
1885-90	77 / 9	66 / 12	87 / 3	95 / 2	77 / 9	82 / 7	82 / 7	83 / 5	85 / 4	83 / 5	100 / 1	. / .	. / .	0 / 13	71 / 10
SYMMETRY OF CONFLICT															
1870-74	75 / 1	0 / 5	60 / 2	. / .	. / .	33 / 4	. / .	. / .	. / .	. / .	50 / 3	. / .	. / .	. / .	. / .
1875-79	20 / 7	67 / 3	83 / 1	25 / 6	. / .	73 / 2	. / .	. / .	33 / 5	0 / 8	57 / 4	. / .	0 / 8	. / .	. / .
1880-84	84 / 5	33 / 10	100 / 1	55 / 6	50 / 7	100 / 1	50 / 7	. / .	. / .	. / .	100 / 1	. / .	0 / 11	100 / 1	50 / 7

TABLE B.4   Time-Periods Legend

1+2	1870 to conclusion of the Three Emperors' League
1+2+3	1870 to conclusion of War-In-Sight Crisis
1+2+3+4	1870 to outbreak of Russo-Turkish War
4+5	Turkish Reforms (1875) to issuing of Congress of Berlin invitations
6	Congress of Berlin to signing of Dual Alliance
7	Attraction of Russia to Dual Alliance to signing of Three Emperors' Alliance
6+7+8	Congress of Berlin to signing of Triple Alliance and British Occupation of Egypt
6+7+8+9	Congress of Berlin to fall of Ferry Government, end of French/ German entente
10+11+12	Uprising in Bulgaria to signing of Second Mediterranean Agreement
13+14+15	End of Bulgarian Uprising, French/Italian war scare to end of 1890
10+11+12+13+14+15	Uprising in Bulgaria to 1890

TABLE B.5 Alignment (Cooperation/Conflict Levels): Total Symmetry*

Time Period	Ger/Brt	Ger/Rus	Ger/Fm	Ger/Aus	Ger/It	Brt/Rus	Brt/Fm	Brt/Aus	Brt/It	Rus/Fm	Rus/Aus	Rus/It	Fm/Aus	Fm/It	Aus/It	Systemic Average
1+2	8 / 54.0	3 / 56.8	14 / 43.5	6 / 54.6	4 / 55.7	5 / 54.7	7 / 54.1	9 / 53.8	1 / 60.1	11 / 53.3	— / 57.0	—	12 / 53.2	13 / 45.6	10 / 53.4	53.2
1+2+3	13 / 47.9	6 / 54.0	15 / 44.1	8 / 53.8	10 / 52.7	2 / 56.4	2 / 56.4	12 / 51.9	11 / 52.0	5 / 55.1	1 / 57.0	2 / 56.4	9 / 52.9	13 / 47.9	7 / 54.7	–
1+2+3+4	12 / 50.2	8 / 53.7	15 / 44.9	1 / 55.3	7 / 53.9	10 / 52.4	3 / 55.9	10 / 52.4	12 / 52.0	6 / 54.2	2 / 57.2	1 / 58.0	5 / 54.4	14 / 47.9	8 / 53.7	52.1
4+5	7 / 53.7	11 / 52.5	13 / 50.1	1 / 58.2	2 / 57.2	15 / 45.8	5 / 55.0	9 / 53.1	14 / 49.3	8 / 51.3	9 / 53.1	3 / 56.7	4 / 56.3	6 / 54.8	12 / 52.0	52.8
6	6 / 53.5	10 / 48.7	5 / 55.3	2 / 58.8	4 / 57.1	9 / 49.7	11 / 51.2	2 / 58.8	13 / 43.2	7 / 52.0	12 / 47.0	11 / 47.4	1 / 59.1	—	—	51.7
7	5 / 54.4	2 / 56.5	3 / 55.0	7 / 53.9	13 / 45.1	9 / 52.5	11 / 49.5	4 / 54.6	6 / 54.2	12 / 47.0	8 / 52.9	—	1 / 61.0	14 / 42.3	10 / 50.6	52.3
6+7+8	3 / 53.9	6 / 52.6	5 / 52.8	1 / 56.2	10 / 50.5	11 / 50.1	8 / 51.9	2 / 55.7	13 / 48.4	9 / 51.2	12 / 49.7	15 / 42.6	7 / 52.0	14 / 44.9	4 / 53.1	53.3
6+7+8+9	8 / 51.6	3 / 53.5	4 / 53.2	5 / 56.3	11 / 50.2	9 / 50.5	13 / 48.9	2 / 53.8	12 / 49.6	7 / 51.4	9 / 50.5	15 / 42.6	6 / 52.2	14 / 43.9	5 / 53.1	52.6
10+11+12	6 / 52.6	7 / 51.1	13 / 46.3	5 / 52.7	3 / 55.7	11 / 46.3	10 / 47.4	4 / 55.2	1 / 58.5	8 / 50.0	12 / 46.0	14 / 41.5	9 / 48.1	15 / 39.7	2 / 57.2	51.0
13+14+15	5 / 54.3	9 / 48.3	12 / 43.1	7 / 52.4	3 / 56.6	10 / 45.5	8 / 50.3	6 / 53.3	4 / 55.5	2 / 57.3	11 / 43.2	15 / 38.9	13 / 42.8	14 / 41.0	1 / 57.5	50.0
10+11+12+ 13+14+15	5 / 53.3	8 / 50.0	12 / 44.5	7 / 52.6	3 / 56.1	10 / 46.1	9 / 48.8	4 / 54.9	1 / 57.5	6 / 53.2	11 / 45.2	14 / 40.7	12 / 44.5	15 / 40.6	2 / 57.3	50.6
SYMMETRY OF CONFLICT																
1+2	3 / 2	5 / 1	1 / 8	—	—	2 / 3	—	—	—	—	3 / 2	—	—	—	—	
1+2+3	2 / 5	3 / 3	1 / 14	—	—	3 / 3	—	—	—	6 / 1	5 / 2	—	6 / 1	—	—	

178

TABLE B.5 (Continued)

Time Period	Ger/Brt	Ger/Rus	Ger/Frn	Ger/Aus	Ger/Itl	Brt/Rus	Brt/Frn	Brt/Aus	Brt/Itl	Rus/Frn	Rus/Aus	Rus/Itl	Frn/Aus	Frn/Itl	Aus/Itl	Systemic Average
1+2+3+4	3 / 7	5 / 4	1 / 16	·	·	2 / 9	·	·	·	6 / 1	4 / 6	·	6 / 1	·	·	
4+5	4 / 2	3 / 3	4 / 2	·	·	1 / 21	·	·	·	·	2 / 6	·	·	·	·	
6	4 / 1	1 / 7	·	3 / 3	·	2 / 5	·	·	4 / 1	·	4 / 1	·	·	·	·	
7	4 / 1	·	·	1 / 7	·	·	·	·	·	·	3 / 2	·	·	2 / 4	·	
6+7+8	8 / 2	1 / 10	11 / 1	1 / 10	8 / 2	3 / 5	8 / 2	·	6 / 3	·	6 / 3	·	·	4 / 4	4 / 4	
6+7+8+9	4 / 8	3 / 10	10 / 15	1 / 15	10 / 1	4 / 8	2 / 12	·	8 / 3	·	8 / 3	·	1 / 12	4 / 1	4 / 7	
10+11+12	6 / 5	1 / 14	3 / 8	2 / 9	8 / 3	4 / 7	9 / 2	10 / 1	·	10 / 1	5 / 6	·	·	·	6 / 5	
13+14+15	3 / 4	1 / 7	·	4 / 1	·	·	4 / 1	·	4 / 1	4 / 1	·	·	·	1 / 7	4 / 1	
10+11+12+ / 13+14+15	3 / 9	1 / 21	3 / 9	2 / 10	9 / 3	6 / 7	10 / 2	11 / 1	11 / 1	·	6 / 7	·	·	5 / 8	8 / 6	

SYMMETRY OF COOPERATION

Time Period	Ger/Brt	Ger/Rus	Ger/Frn	Ger/Aus	Ger/Itl	Brt/Rus	Brt/Frn	Brt/Aus	Brt/Itl	Rus/Frn	Rus/Aus	Rus/Itl	Frn/Aus	Frn/Itl	Aus/Itl	Systemic Average
1+2	5 / 2	3 / 4	6 / 1	1 / 5	·	6 / 1	4 / 3	·	·	·	1 / 5	·	·	·	·	
1+2+3	9 / 2	3 / 5	6 / 4	3 / 5	·	8 / 3	2 / 6	·	·	1 / 9	3 / 5	·	9 / 2	·	6 / 4	
1+2+3+4	4 / 11	2 / 15	7 / 8	4 / 11	·	6 / 10	8 / 6	10 / 5	·	3 / 13	1 / 22	·	11 / 4	·	8 / 6	
4+5	4 / 13	5 / 12	7 / 9	6 / 10	·	3 / 14	10 / 3	2 / 16	·	8 / 4	1 / 20	·	8 / 4	·	·	
6	2 / 7	2 / 7	·	1 / 13	·	2 / 7	·	5 / 5	6 / 2	·	6 / 2	·	·	·	·	

(Table B.5 continues on page 180)

TABLE B.5 (Continued)

Time Period	Ger/ Brt	Ger/ Rus	Ger/ Frn	Ger/ Aus	Ger/ Itl	Brt/ Rus	Brt/ Frn	Brt/ Aus	Brt/ Itl	Rus/ Frn	Rus/ Aus	Rus/ Itl	Frn/ Aus	Frn/ Itl	Aus/ Itl	Systemic Average
7	3 / 10	2 / 21	- / -	1 / 32	- / -	- / -	- / -	5 / 5	- / -	- / -	4 / 6	- / -	- / -	6 / 4	- / -	
6+7+8	3 / 20	2 / 28	11 / 3	1 / 35	7 / 8	7 / 8	4 / 15	6 / 10	12 / 1	- / -	7 / 8	- / -	- / -	10 / 6	4 / 15	
6+7+8+9	3 / 27	2 / 32	7 / 13	1 / 43	10 / 9	4 / 19	5 / 17	8 / 12	13 / 2	12 / 3	8 / 12	- / -	13 / 2	11 / 6	6 / 15	
10+11+12	2 / 17	1 / 22	8 / 6	3 / 16	7 / 14	10 / 7	11 / 3	3 / 16	3 / 16	9 / 4	12 / 2	- / -	- / -	- / -	6 / 15	
13+14+15	1 / 14	3 / 10	- / -	7 / 3	2 / 12	- / -	4 / 8	- / -	7 / 3	4 / 8	- / -	- / -	- / -	- / -	6 / 6	
10+11+12+ 13+14+15	2 / 31	1 / 32	10 / 7	5 / 19	3 / 26	10 / 7	9 / 11	7 / 18	5 / 19	8 / 12	12 / 2	- / -	- / -	- / -	4 / 21	

*The first row of numbers in each time period is the rank of the dyad; the second row is the cooperation/conflict level. For the key to the time periods, see page 177.

Abbreviations: Ger = Germany, Brt = Great Britain, Rus = Russia, Frn = France, Itl = Italy, Aus = Austria-Hungary.

TABLE B.6   Symmetry of Interactions, by Time Periods (Total Dyad): Total Symmetry*

Time Periods	Ger/Brt		Ger/Rus		Ger/Frn		Ger/Aus		Ger/Itl		Brt/Rus		Brt/Frn		Brt/Aus		Brt/Itl		Rus/Frn		Rus/Aus		Frn/Aus		Frn/Itl		Aus/Itl	
1+2	1	75	3	60	5	56	3	60	-	-	6	50	-	-	-	-	-	-	-	-	2	71	-	-	-	-	-	-
1+2+3	3	71	9	50	5	67	7	60	-	-	5	67	1	83	-	-	-	-	7	60	3	71	10	33	-	-	2	75
1+2+3+4	7	61	10	47	2	75	5	73	-	-	4	74	1	83	11	20	-	-	9	50	2	75	8	60	-	-	6	67
4+5	6	60	7	53	1	100	3	90	-	-	4	71	-	-	8	38	7	33	9	25	5	62	1	100	-	-	-	-
6	3	88	4	71	-	-	5	67	-	-	2	92	-	-	1	100	-	-	-	-	6	67	-	-	3	88	-	-
7	5	55	2	90	-	-	6	36	-	-	-	-	-	-	4	60	-	-	-	-	6	100	-	-	3	90	-	-
6+7+8	9	68	6	79	7	75	8	69	11	30	1	92	4	82	5	80	12	25	-	-	2	91	-	-	1	90	10	47
6+7+8+9	10	60	4	76	9	64	5	71	14	27	3	85	8	66	6	67	12	40	6	67	2	87	13	33	1	90	11	47
10+11+12	6	68	11	58	5	71	3	80	7	65	2	86	10	60	4	76	1	88	12	40	9	63	-	-	-	-	7	65
13+14+15	6	67	9	47	-	-	1	100	5	83	-	-	3	89	-	-	8	50	3	89	-	-	-	-	1	100	7	57
10+11+12+ 13+14+15	10	68	13	55	7	75	3	83	8	72	2	86	5	79	5	79	4	80	9	71	11	67	-	-	1	100	12	63
SYMMETRY OF COOPERATION																												
1+2	1	100	4	75	-	-	6	60	-	-	1	100	5	67	-	-	-	-	-	-	3	80	-	-	-	-	-	-
1+2+3	1	100	8	60	5	75	8	60	-	-	1	100	3	83	-	-	-	-	7	67	4	80	10	50	-	-	5	75
1+2+3+4	8	64	10	47	2	88	6	73	-	-	1	90	3	83	11	20	-	-	9	54	4	77	5	75	-	-	7	67
4+5	7	62	8	50	1	100	3	90	-	-	4	71	5	67	9	38	4	80	10	25	6	65	1	100	-	-	-	-
6	1	100	5	71	-	-	4	85	-	-	1	100	-	-	1	100	-	-	-	-	6	50	-	-	-	-	-	-
7	5	60	2	90	-	-	4	69	-	-	-	-	-	-	5	60	-	-	-	-	1	100	-	-	3	75	-	-

(Table B.6 continues on page 182)

TABLE B.6 (Continued)

Time Periods	Ger/Brt	Ger/Rus	Ger/Frm	Ger/Aus	Ger/Itl	Brt/Rus	Brt/Frm	Brt/Aus	Brt/Itl	Rus/Frm	Rus/Aus	Frm/Aus	Frm/Itl	Aus/Itl
6+7+8	8 75	3 86	9 67	5 80	11 25	1 100	5 80	5 80	12 0	8 67	2 88	11 —	4 83	10 47
6+7+8+9	10 56	1 88	7 73	5 79	14 22	2 84	6 76	6 67	11 50	— 50	3 83	— 50	3 83	13 47
10+11+12	7 76	11 64	5 83	3 94	9 71	1 100	10 67	6 81	4 88	12 50	1 100	— —	— —	8 73
13+14+15	5 79	6 70	— —	1 100	4 83	— —	3 88	— —	7 67	1 100	— —	— —	— —	6 67
10+11+12+ 13+14+15	9 77	12 66	4 86	3 95	9 77	1 100	8 82	6 83	5 84	6 83	1 100	— —	— —	11 71
SYMMETRY OF CONFLICT														
1+2	2 50	5 0	1 63	— —	— —	4 33	— —	— —	— —	— —	2 50	— —	— —	— —
1+2+3	2 60	4 33	1 64	— —	— —	4 33	— —	— —	— —	6 0	3 50	6 0	— —	— —
1+2+3+4	3 57	5 50	1 69	— —	— —	4 56	— —	— —	— —	6 0	2 67	6 0	— —	— —
4+5	4 50	3 67	1 100	— —	— —	2 71	— —	— —	— —	— —	4 50	— —	— —	— —
6	5 0	3 71	— —	5 0	— —	2 80	— —	— —	4 33	— —	1 100	— —	— —	— —
7	4 0	4 —	— —	3 43	— —	— —	— —	— —	— —	— —	1 100	— —	1 100	— —
6+7+8	11 0	6 60	1 100	10 30	7 50	5 80	1 100	— —	9 33	— —	1 100	12 0	1 100	7 50
6+7+8+9	5 75	6 60	1 100	10 47	7 50	4 88	7 50	— —	11 33	— —	1 100	— —	1 100	7 50
10+11+12	7 40	4 50	2 63	3 56	9 33	1 71	4 50	10 0	— —	10 0	4 50	— —	— —	7 40
13+14+15	4 25	5 14	— —	1 100	— —	— —	1 100	— —	6 0	6 0	— —	— —	1 100	6 0
10+11+12+ 13+14+15	8 33	7 38	3 67	5 60	8 33	2 71	3 67	11 0	11 0	11 0	6 57	— —	1 100	10 30

*In each dyad column, the first figure is the rank of the dyad; the second figure is the symmetry percentage. Due to lack of interactions, there is no dyad column for Russia/Italy. For key to time periods, see page 177.

Abbreviations: Ger = Germany; Brt = Great Britain; Frm = France; Aus = Austria-Hungary; Itl = Italy; Rus = Russia.

TABLE B.7 Alliance (Dependence/Independence)—Number of Dyadic Alliance Months*

Time Period	Germany/ Britain	Germany/ Russia	Germany/ Aus-Hun	Germany/ Italy	Britain/ Aus-Hun	Britain/ Italy	Russia/ Aus-Hun	Aus-Hun/ Italy
1870-73	-	-	-	-	-	-	-	-
1873-75	-	15	15	-	-	-	15	-
1874-76	-	18	18	-	-	-	18	-
1875-77	-	18	18	-	-	-	24	-
1876-78	-	15	15	-	-	-	24	-
1877-79	-	9	11	-	-	-	18	-
1878-80	-	3	17	-	-	-	6	-
1879-81	-	3	29	-	-	-	3	-
1880-82	-	9	52	-	-	-	9	-
1881-83	-	15	72	19	-	-	15	19
1882-84	-	18	99	31	-	-	18	31
1883-85	-	18	116	36	-	-	18	36
1884-86	-	18	126	36	-	-	18	36
1885-87	3.5	18	123	39.5	3.5	5	15	39.5
1886-88	9.5	18	117	63.5	15.5	17	9	58.5
1887-89	15.5	18	111	93.5	27.5	29	3	82.5
1888-90	18	18	108	120	36	36	-	103

*Dyads not listed have no alliance months.

TABLE B.8   Military Dimension, Three Variables (Percentage Shares)

Time Period	Germany	Britain	Russia	Austria-Hungary	France	Italy
1870-73	9.7	19.6	24.7	9.2	26.6	10.2
1873-75	12.7	20.7	24.5	9.2	24.7	8.2
1874-76	13.2	21.3	24.3	9.2	24.6	7.3
1875-77	13.7	20.7	24.5	9.2	24.5	7.5
1876-78	14.0	21.3	24.1	9.1	23.7	7.8
1877-79	14.3	21.0	24.1	9.0	23.6	7.9
1878-80	14.0	21.0	24.0	9.3	23.6	7.9
1879-81	14.4	20.4	24.5	9.2	23.4	8.1
1880-82	14.9	20.1	24.0	9.4	23.4	8.2
1881-83	15.3	19.9	23.1	9.5	23.6	8.6
1882-84	15.5	19.8	22.3	9.4	23.7	9.2
1883-85	15.3	20.3	22.2	9.2	23.3	9.7
1884-86	15.2	20.9	22.9	9.0	22.0	10.0
1885-87	15.9	21.3	22.3	8.9	21.5	10.0
1886-88	16.8	21.3	21.9	9.1	20.6	10.4
1887-89	17.3	20.4	21.6	9.4	20.9	10.3
1888-90	17.7	19.7	21.9	9.5	21.0	10.3

TABLE B.9 Industrial and Mobilization Dimension, Seven Variables (Percentage Shares)

Time Period	Germany	Britain	Russia	Austria-Hungary	France	Italy
1870-73	19.5	42.2	10.6	8.7	16.6	6.1
1873-75	20.4	40.4	10.9	9.0	17.1	6.0
1874-76	21.4	42.3	11.1	9.3	17.7	6.0
1875-77	20.3	40.3	11.1	9.1	16.9	6.0
1876-78	20.5	40.0	11.4	9.2	16.5	6.0
1877-79	20.9	39.1	12.1	9.2	16.7	5.9
1878-80	21.2	38.4	12.7	9.0	16.7	5.0
1879-81	21.4	38.3	12.7	8.9	16.6	5.0
1880-82	21.2	37.3	12.2	8.8	15.6	5.0
1881-83	21.6	37.2	12.0	8.9	15.5	4.8
1882-84	22.3	36.6	12.0	9.2	15.6	4.5
1883-85	22.8	35.9	12.0	9.2	15.4	4.6
1884-86	23.3	37.5	12.1	9.2	15.0	4.7
1885-87	23.5	35.7	12.2	8.9	14.6	4.9
1886-88	23.7	35.8	12.3	8.9	14.3	5.0
1887-89	23.5	36.4	13.2	9.6	15.1	5.5
1888-90	23.8	35.8	13.4	9.7	15.2	5.4

TABLE B.10   Combined Power Index, Ten Variables (Percentage Shares)

Time Period	Germany	Britain	Russia	Austria-Hungary	France	Italy
1870-73	16.2	35.4	14.8	8.8	19.6	7.5
1873-75	17.9	34.5	15.0	9.0	19.4	6.7
1874-76	18.7	36.0	15.1	9.3	19.8	6.4
1875-77	18.1	34.5	15.1	9.1	19.2	6.5
1876-78	18.3	34.4	15.2	9.2	18.7	6.6
1877-79	18.7	33.7	15.7	9.1	18.8	6.6
1878-80	18.8	33.2	16.1	9.1	18.8	5.9
1879-81	19.1	32.0	16.3	9.0	18.6	5.9
1880-82	19.3	32.2	15.9	9.0	18.0	5.9
1881-83	19.7	32.0	15.3	9.0	17.9	5.9
1882-84	20.2	31.5	15.1	9.2	18.0	5.9
1883-85	20.6	31.3	15.1	9.2	17.8	6.1
1884-86	20.9	31.2	15.4	9.2	17.1	6.3
1885-87	21.2	31.4	15.2	8.9	16.7	6.5
1886-88	21.6	31.4	15.2	9.0	16.2	6.6
1887-89	21.5	31.6	15.7	9.6	16.8	7.0
1888-90	21.8	31.0	16.0	9.7	17.0	6.9

TABLE B.11 Status—Ascribed Status (Diplomatic Recognitions Plus Diplomatic Representations), Percentage Shares

Time Period	Germany	Britain	Russia	Austria-Hungary	France	Italy
1870-73	17.3	24.7	10.8	13.0	18.2	16.1
1873-75	17.4	24.3	10.5	13.8	18.2	15.9
1874-76	17.1	24.2	10.4	14.1	18.0	16.2
1875-77	16.9	24.3	10.4	14.2	18.0	16.4
1876-78	16.9	24.3	10.4	14.3	18.1	16.3
1877-79	17.4	23.9	10.3	14.2	18.1	16.2
1878-80	16.9	23.9	11.0	14.4	17.6	16.3
1879-81	16.8	23.4	11.2	14.2	18.4	16.1
1880-82	16.6	23.4	11.4	14.2	18.4	16.1
1881-83	16.3	23.6	11.6	14.3	18.5	15.9
1882-84	16.0	23.6	11.8	14.3	18.8	15.3
1883-85	15.6	23.8	11.7	14.3	18.6	15.7
1884-86	15.9	23.8	11.7	14.1	18.9	15.8
1885-87	15.9	23.8	11.7	13.8	18.9	16.0
1886-88	16.0	23.9	11.7	13.9	18.5	16.1
1887-89	15.9	24.2	11.9	13.9	18.4	15.9
1888-90	16.1	24.1	12.1	13.8	18.4	15.7

TABLE B.12 Status—Achieved Status (Combined Power Index), Percentage Shares

Time Period	Germany	Britain	Russia	Austria-Hungary	France	Italy
1870-73	16.2	35.4	14.8	8.8	19.6	7.5
1873-75	17.9	34.5	15.0	9.0	19.4	6.7
1874-76	18.7	36.0	15.1	9.3	19.8	6.4
1875-77	18.1	34.5	15.1	9.1	19.2	6.5
1876-78	18.3	34.4	15.2	9.2	18.7	6.6
1877-79	18.7	33.7	15.7	9.1	18.8	6.6
1878-80	18.8	33.2	16.1	9.1	18.8	5.9
1879-81	19.1	32.0	16.3	9.0	18.6	5.9
1880-82	19.3	32.2	15.9	9.0	18.0	5.9
1881-83	19.7	32.0	15.3	9.0	17.9	5.9
1882-84	20.2	31.5	15.1	9.2	18.0	5.9
1883-85	20.6	31.3	15.1	9.2	17.8	6.1
1884-86	20.9	31.2	15.4	9.2	17.1	6.3
1885-87	21.2	31.4	15.2	8.9	16.7	6.5
1886-88	21.6	31.4	15.2	9.0	16.2	6.6
1887-89	21.5	31.6	15.7	9.6	16.8	7.0
1888-90	21.8	31.0	16.0	9.7	17.0	6.9

TABLE B.13 Status Rank—Joint Status (Achieved Plus Ascribed), Percentage Shares

Time Period	Germany	Britain	Russia	Austria-Hungary	France	Italy
1870-73	16.8	30.1	72.8	10.9	18.9	11.8
1873-75	17.7	29.4	12.8	11.4	18.8	11.3
1874-76	17.9	30.1	12.8	11.7	18.9	11.3
1875-77	17.5	29.4	12.8	11.7	18.6	11.5
1876-78	17.6	29.4	12.8	11.8	18.4	11.5
1877-79	18.1	28.8	13.0	11.7	18.5	11.4
1878-80	17.9	28.6	13.6	11.8	18.2	11.1
1879-81	18.0	28.2	13.8	11.6	18.5	11.0
1880-82	18.0	27.8	13.2	11.6	18.2	11.0
1881-83	18.0	27.8	13.5	11.7	18.2	10.9
1882-84	18.1	27.6	13.5	11.8	18.2	10.9
1883-85	18.1	27.6	13.4	11.8	18.2	10.9
1884-86	18.4	27.5	13.6	11.7	18.2	11.1
1885-87	18.6	27.6	13.5	11.4	18.0	11.3
1886-88	18.8	27.7	13.5	11.5	17.8	11.4
1887-89	18.7	27.9	13.8	11.8	17.6	11.5
1888-90	19.0	27.6	14.1	11.8	17.7	11.3

TABLE B.14 Status Inconsistency (Percentage Share Difference)

Time Period	Germany	Britain	Russia	Austria-Hungary	France	Italy
1870-73	-1.1	+10.7	+4.0	- 4.2	+1.4	- 8.6
1873-75	+0.5	+10.2	+4.5	- 4.8	+1.2	-11.2
1874-76	+1.6	+11.8	+4.7	- 4.8	+1.8	- 9.8
1875-77	+1.2	+10.2	+4.7	- 5.1	+1.2	- 9.9
1876-78	+1.4	+10.1	+4.8	- 5.1	+0.6	- 9.7
1877-79	+1.3	+ 9.8	+5.4	- 5.1	+0.7	- 9.6
1878-80	+1.9	+ 9.3	+5.1	- 5.3	+1.2	-10.4
1879-81	+2.3	+ 9.6	+5.1	- 5.2	+0.2	-10.2
1880-82	+2.7	+ 8.8	+4.5	- 5.2	- 0.4	-10.2
1881-83	+3.4	+ 8.4	+3.7	- 5.3	- 0.6	-10.0
1882-84	+4.2	+ 7.9	+3.3	- 5.1	- 0.8	- 9.4
1883-85	+5.0	+ 7.5	+3.4	- 5.1	- 0.8	- 9.6
1884-86	+5.0	+ 7.4	+3.7	- 4.9	- 1.8	- 9.5
1885-87	+5.3	+ 7.6	+3.5	- 4.9	- 2.2	- 9.5
1886-88	+5.6	+ 7.5	+3.5	- 4.9	- 2.3	- 9.5
1887-89	+5.6	+ 7.4	+3.8	- 4.3	- 1.6	- 8.9
1888-90	+5.7	+ 6.9	+3.9	- 4.1	- 1.4	- 8.8

*Achieved > Ascribed = (+)
 Ascribed > Achieved = (-)

REFERENCES

ALEXANDROFF, A. S. (1979) "Symmetry in international relations: an empirical analysis of the behavioral interaction of the european powers from 1870-1890. Ph.D. dissertation, Cornell University.
——— R. ROSECRANCE, and A. STEIN (1977) "History, quantitative analysis, and the balance of power." Journal of Conflict Resolution 21: 35-56.
ASHWORTH, W. (1966) An Economic History of England 1870-1939. London: Methuen.
AXELROD, R. [ed.] (1976) Structure of Decision: The Cognitive Maps of Political Elites. Princeton, NJ: Princeton University Press.
——— (1977) "Argumentation in foreign policy settings: Britain in 1918, Munich in 1938, and Japan in 1970. Journal of Conflict Resolution 21: 727-744.
——— (1980) "Effective choices in the prisoner's dilemma. Journal of Conflict Resolution 24: 3-26.
AZAR, E. E., R. A. BRODY, and C. McCLELLAND (1972) "International Events Interaction Analysis: Some Research Considerations." Sage Professional Papers in International Studies, 1, 02-001. Beverly Hills and London: Sage Publications.
BALDWIN, D. (1971a) "The costs of power." Journal of Conflict Resolution 15: 145-155.
——— (1971b) "The power of positive sanctions." World Politics 24: 19-38.
——— (1971c) "Inter-nation influence revisited." Journal of Conflict Resolution 15: 471-486.
BISMARCK, O. von (1899/1966) Bismarck: The Man and the Statesman. Being the Reflections and Reminiscences of Otto, Prince von Bismarck. Written an Dictated by Himself after His Retirement from Office. (J. Butler, trans.). New York: Harper and Brothers reprinted New York: Howard Fertig.
BLACKWELL, W. (1970) The Industrialization of Russia: An Historical Perspective. New York: Thomas Y. Crowell.
BLAU, P. M. (1964) Exchange and Power in Social Life. New York: John Wiley.
BOULDING, K. (1969) "National images and international systems," pp. 442-431 in J. Rosenau (ed.) International Politics and Foreign Policy, Second Edition. New York: Free Press.
BRAMS, S. (1969) "The Structure of influence relationships in the international system," pp. 583-599 in J. Rosenau (ed.) International Politics and Foreign Policy: A Reader in Research and Theory. New York: Free Press.

BREMER, S. (1980) "National capabilities and war proneness," pp. 57-82 in J. D. Singer (ed.) The Correlates of War: II. Beverly Hills: Sage Publications.

BROWN, S. (1979) The Crises of Power: An Interpretation of United States Foreign Policy During the Kissinger Years. New York: Columbia University Press.

BURROWES, R. (1974) "Mirror, mirror, on the wall . . . a comparison of event data sources," pp. 383-406 in J. N. Rosenau (ed.) Comparing Foreign Policies: Theories, Findings, and Methods. New York: John Wiley.

BUTTERFIELD, H. and M. WIGHT [eds.] (1966) Diplomatic Investigations. Essays in the Theory of International Politics. London: George, Allen & Unwin.

CHADWICK-JONES, J. K. (1976) Social Exchange Theory: Its Structure and Influence in Social Psychology. London: Academic.

CHOUCRI, N. and R. C. NORTH (1972) "Dynamics of international conflict: some policy implications of population, resources and technology," pp. 80-122 in R. Tanter and R. H. Ullman (eds.) Theory and Policy in International Relations. Princeton, NJ: Princeton University Press.

——— (1975) Nations in Conflict: National Growth and International Violence. San Francisco: Freeman.

DAHL, R. (1957) "The concept of power." Behavioral Science 2: 201-215.

DEUTSCH, M. (1958) "Trust and suspicion," Journal of Conflict Resolution 3: 265-279.

——— (1973) The Resolution of Conflict: Constructive and Destructive Processes. New Haven, CT: Yale University Press.

EAST, M. (1972) "Status discrepancy and violence in the international system: an empirical analysis," pp. 299-319 in J. Rosenau et al. (eds.) The Analysis of International Politics. New York: Free Press.

EAST, M., S. SALMORE, C. HERMANN (1978) Why Nations Act: Theoretical Perspectives for Comparative Foreign Policy Studies. Beverly Hills: Sage Publications.

EYCK, E. (1950) Bismarck and the German Empire. New York: Norton.

FAY, S. B. (1930) The Origins of the World War. New York: Macmillan.

FERRIS, W. H. (1973) The Power Capabilities of Nation-States: International Conflict and War. Lexington, MA: Lexington.

FRIEDMAN, J., C. BLADEN, and S. ROSEN (1970) Alliance in International Politics. Boston: Allyn & Bacon.

GALTUNG, J. (1966a) "International relations and international conflicts: a sociological approach." Transactions of the sixth World Congress of Sociology, International Sociological Association 1: 121-161.

——— (1966b) "Rank and Social Integration: A Multidimensional Approach," pp. 145-198 in M. Zeldlitch and B. Anderson (eds.) Sociological Theories in Progress, Volume 1. New York: Houghton Mifflin.

——— (1971) "A structural theory of imperialism." Journal of Peace Research 8: 81-117.

GARRETT, B. (1979) "China policy and the strategic triangle," pp. 228-263 in K. Oye et al. (eds) Eagle Entangled: U.S. Foreign Policy in a Complex World. New York: Longman.

GEISS, I. (1976) German Foreign Policy, 1871-1914. Boston: Routledge and Kegan Paul.

GOCHMAN, C. (1980) "Status, capabilities, and major power conflict," pp. 83-123 in J. D. Singer (ed.) The Correlates of War: II Testing Some Realpolitik Models. New York: Free Press.

GOODMAN, R., J. HART, and R. ROSECRANCE (1975) "Testing international theory: methods and data in a situational analysis of international politics," pp. 41-56 in E. E. Azar and J. D. Ben-Dak (eds.) Theory and Practice of Events Research. New York: Gordon & Breach.

GULICK, E. V. (1955) Europe's Classical Balance of Power: A Case History of the Theory and Practice of One of the Great Concepts of European Statecraft. Ithaca, NY: Cornell University Press.

HAMEROW, T. S. [eds.] (1972) Otto von Bismarck: An Historical Assissment, Second Edition. Lexington: D. C. Heath.

HARSANYI, J. C. (1962) "Measurement of social power, opportunity costs, and the theory of 2-person bargaining games." Behavioral Science 7: 67-80.

HART, J. (1974) "Symmetry and polarization in the european international system, 1870-1879: a methodological study." Journal of Peace Research 11: 229-244.

HEALY, B. and A. STEIN (1973) "The balance of power in international history: theory and reality." Journal of Conflict Resolution 17: 33-62.

HERMANN, M. (1980) "Explaining foreign policy behavior using the personal characteristics of political leaders." International Studies Quarterly 24: 7-46.

HILTON, G. (1970) "The 1914 studies—a reassessment of the evidence and some further thoughts." Peace Research Society (International) Papers 13: 117-141.

HINSLEY, F. H. (1963) Power and the Pursuit of Peace: Theory and Practice in the History of Relations Between States. Cambridge: Cambridge University Press.

HOFFMANN, S. (1978) Primacy or World Order. New York: McGraw-Hill.

HOMANS, G. C. (1951) The Human Group. London: Routledge and Kegan Paul.

——— (1961) Social Behavior: Its Elementary Forms. London; Routledge and Kegan Paul.

HOLSTI, O. R. (1972) Crisis Escalation, War. Montreal: McGill-Queen's University Press.

HOLSTI, O. R., R. NORTH, and R. BRODY (1968) "Perception and action in the 1914 crisis," pp. 123-158 in J. D. Singer (ed.) Quantitative International Politics: Insights and Evidence. New York: Free Press.

HOLSTI, O. R., P. T. HOPMANN, and J. D. SULLIVAN (1973) Unity and Disintegration in International Alliances: Comparative Studies. New York: John Wiley.

HOOLE, F. W. and D. A. ZINNES [eds.] (1976) Quantitative International Politics: An Appraisal. New York: Praeger.

IKLÉ, F. C. (1971) Every War Must End. New York: Columbia University Press.

JERVIS, R., (1970) The Logic of Images in International Relations. Princeton, NJ: Princeton University Press.

——— (1972) "Bargaining and bargaining tactics," pp. 272-288 in J. Pennock and J. Chapman (eds.) Coercion. Chicago: Aldine.

——— (1976) Perception and Misperception in International Politics. Princeton, NJ: Princeton University Press.

KAPLAN, M. (1957) System and Process in International Politics. New York: John Wiley.

KAPLOWITZ, S. (1973) "An experimental test of a rationalistic theory of deterrence." Journal of Conflict Resolution 27: 535-572.

KELLEY, E. W. (1978a) Doing Political Science. (unpublished)
——— (1978b) Cause in Political Science. (unpublished)
KELMAN, H. C. [eds.] (1965) International Behavior: A Social-Psychological Analysis. New York: Holt, Rinehart & Winston.
KEMP, T. (1971) Economic Forces in French History: An Essay on the Development of the French Economy 1760-1914. London: Dennis Dobson.
KISSINGER, H. (1968) "The white revolutionary: reflection on Bismarck." Daedalus (Summer): 888-924.
KNORR, K. (1975) The Power of Nations: The Political Economy of International Relations. New York: Basic Books.
LANGER, W. (1964) European Alliances and Alignments 1871-1890. New York: Vintage.
——— (1972) An Encyclopedia of World History, Fifth Edition. Boston: Houghton Mifflin.
——— (1978) The Diplomacy of Imperialism, 1890-1902, Second Edition. New York: Knopf.
LENG, R. J. (1972) "Coder's manual for identifying and describing international actions." Middlebury College. (mimeo)
——— (1973) "The future of events data marriages: a question of compatibility." Paper presented at the meetings of the International Studies Association, New York, March 13-16.
——— (1980) "Influence strategies and interstate conflict," pp. 124-160 in J. D. Singer (ed.) The Correlates of War: II Testing Some Realpolitik Models. New York: Free Press.
LENG, R. and R. GOODSELL (1974) "Behavioral indicators of war proneness in bilateral conflicts," pp. 191-226 in P. J. McGowen (ed.) Sage International Yearbook of Foreign Policy, Volume II. Beverly Hills: Sage Publications.
LENG, R. J. and J. D. SINGER (1970) "Toward a multi-theoretical typology of international behavior." Ann Arbor, MI: Mental Health Research Institute. (mimeo)
LENG, R. and H. WHEELER (1979) "Influence strategies, success, and war." Journal of Conflict Resolution 23: 655-684.
LEVY, A. (1977) "Coder's manual for identifying serious inter-nation disputes, 1816-1965." Correlates of War Project Internal Memo. Ann Arbor, Michigan.
LEWIN, K. (1951) Field Theory in Social Science: Selected Theoretical Papers. New York: Harper & Row.
LOCKHART, C. (1973) "The Efficiency of Threats in International Interaction Strategies." Sage Professional Papers in International Studies, 2, 02-023. Beverly Hills: Sage Publications.
——— (1977) "Problems in the management and resolution of international conflicts." World Politics 29: 370-403.
——— (1979) Bargaining in International Conflicts. New York: Columbia University Press.
McCLELLAND, C. (1961) "The acute international crisis," pp. 182-204 in K. Knorr (ed.) The International System: Theoretical Essays. Princeton, NJ: Princeton University Press.

——— (1962) "The reorientation of the sociology of conflict: a review." Journal of Conflict Resolution 6: 88-95.

——— (1966) Theory and the International System. New York: Macmillan.

——— (1968) "Access to Berlin: the quantity and variety of events, 1948-1963," pp. 159-186 in J. D. Singer (ed.) Quantitative International Politics: Insights and Evidence. New York: Free Press.

——— (1972) "The beginning, duration, and abatement of international crises," pp. 83-108 in C. F. Hermann (ed.) International Crises: Insights from Behavioral Research. New York: Free Press.

McCLELLAND, C. and G. HOGGARD (1969) "Conflict patterns in the interactions among nations," pp. 714-724 in J. Rosenau (ed.) International Politics and Foreign Policy: A Reader in Research and Theory, Revised Edition. New York: Free Press.

MEDLICOTT, W. N. (1965) Bismarck and Modern Germany, New York: Harper & Row.

MIDLARSKY, M. (1969) "Status inconsistency and the onset of international warfare." Ph.D. dissertation, Northwestern University.

MITCHELL, P. B. (1935) The Bismarckian Policy of Conciliation With France. Philadelphia: University of Pennsylvania Press.

MOSES, L. E., R. A. BRODY, O. R. HOLSTI, J. B. KADANE, and J. S. MILSTEIN (1967) "Scaling data on inter-nation action." Science 156: 1054-1059.

NORTH, R. (1977) "Toward a framework for the analysis of scarcity and conflict." International Studies Quarterly 21: 569-592.

ORGANSKI, A.F.K. (1958) World Politics. New York: Knopf.

——— (1968) World Politics, Second Edition. New York: Knopf.

PETERSON, S. (1975) "Research on research: events data studies, 1961-72," pp. 263-310 in P. McGowan (ed.) Sage International Yearbook of Foreign Policy Studies, Volume 3. Beverly Hills: Sage Publications.

PFLANZE, O. (1976) "Bismarck's Realpolitik," pp. 155-180 in J. Sheehan (ed.) Imperial Germany. New York: New Viewpoints.

PHILLIPS, W. R. (1971) "The dynamics of behavioral action and reaction in international conflict." Peace Research Society (International) Papers 17: 31-46.

——— (1973) "The conflict environment of nations: a study of conflict inputs to nations in 1963," pp. 124-147 in J. Wilkenfeld (ed.) Conflict Behavior and Linkage Politics. New York: McKay.

PHILLIPS, W. R. and R. C. CRAIN (1974) "Dynamic foreign policy interactions: reciprocity and uncertainty in foreign policy," pp. 227-268 in P. McGowan (ed.) Sage International Yearbook of Foreign Policy Studies, Volume Two. Beverly Hills: Sage Publications.

PRUITT, D. (1965) "Definition of the situation as a determinant of international action," pp. 393-432 in H. Kelman (ed.) International Behavior: A Social-Psychological Analysis. New York: Holt, Rinehart & Winston.

RAPOPORT, A. (1960) Fights, Games, and Debates. Ann Arbor: University of Michigan Press.

RAPOPORT, A., M. GUYER, and D. GORDON (1976) The 2 x 2 Game. Ann Arbor: University of Michigan Press.

ROHL, J. (1970) From Bismarck to Hitler: The Problem of Continuity in German History. London: Longam.

ROSECRANCE, R. N. (1963) Action and Reaction in World Politics: International Systems in Perspective. Boston: Little, Brown.

——— (1968) "Diplomacy," pp. 187-191 in D. Sills (ed.) International Encyclopedia of the Social Sciences, Volume Four. New York: Free Press.

——— P. DeLEON, and J. MacQUEEN (1969) "Research report: situational analysis in international politics." Behavioral Science 14: 51-58.

ROSECRANCE, R. N., A. ALEXANDROFF, B. HEALY, and A. STEIN (1974) "Power, Balance of Power, and Status in Nineteenth Century International Relations." Sage Professional Papers in International Studies, 3, 02-029. Beverly Hills and London: Sage Publications.

RUMMEL, R. J. (1963) "Dimensions of conflict behavior within and between nations." General Systems Yearbook 8: 1-50.

——— (1964) "Testing some possible predictors of conflict behavior within and between nations." Peace Research Society (International) Papers 1: 79-111.

——— (1968) "The relationship between national attributes and foreign conflict behavior," pp. 187-214 in J. D. Singer (ed.) Quantitative International Politics. New York: Free Press.

——— (1971) "A status-field theory of international relations." Dimensionability of Nations Project Research Report 50, University of Hawaii.

——— (1972) Dimensions of Nations. Beverly Hills: Sage Publications.

——— (1975) The Dynamic Psychological Field. Beverly Hills: Sage Publications.

——— (1977) Field Theory Evolving. Beverly Hills: Sage Publications.

RUSSETT, B. [ed.] (1972) Peace, War, and Numbers. Beverly Hills: Sage Publications.

——— (1974) "An empirical typology of international military alliances," pp. 301-324 in B. M. Russett (ed.) Power and Community in World Politics. San Francisco: Freeman.

SCHMITT, B. E. (1934) Triple Alliance and Triple Entente. New York: Henry Holt.

SCHROEDER, P. W. (1976) "Alliances, 1815-1914: weapons of power and tools of management," pp. 227-262 in K. Knorr (ed.) Historical Dimensions of National Security Problems. Lawrence: University Press of Kansas.

——— (1977) "quantitative studies in the balance of power: an historian's reaction," Journal of Conflict Resolution 21: 3-22.

SHURE, G., R. MEEKER, and E. HAMSFORD (1965) "The effectiveness of pacifist strategies in bargaining games." Journal of Conflict Resolution 9: 106-117.

SINGER, J. D. (1963) "Inter-nation influence: a formal model." American Political Science Review 57: 420-431.

SINGER, J. D. [ed.] (1960) Quantitative International Politics: Insights and Evidence. New York: Free Press.

——— (1969) "The incompleat theorist: insight without evidence," pp. 62-86 in K. Knorr and J. N. Rosenau (eds.) Contending Approaches to International Politics. Princeton, NJ: Princeton University Press.

——— (1974) "The historical experiment as a research strategy in the study of world politics." Political Inquiry 2, 1: 23-52.

––– (1976) "The correlates of war project: continuity, diversity, and convergence," pp. 21-42 in F. Hoole and D. Zinnes (eds.) Quantitative International Politics. New York: Praeger.

SINGER, J. D. and M. SMALL (1966) "Formal alliances, 1815-1939: a quantitative description." Journal of Peace Research 1: 1-32.

SINGER, J. D., S. BREMER, and J. STUCKEY (1972) "Capability distribution, uncertainty, and major power war, 1820-1965," pp. 19-48 in B. M. Russett (ed.) Peace, War and Numbers. Beverly Hills: Sage Publications.

SONTAG, R. J. (1933) European Diplomatic History, 1871-1932. New York: Appleton-Century.

SNYDER, G. (1961) Deterrence and Defense: Toward a Theory of National Security. Princeton, NJ: Princeton University Press.

SNYDER, G. and P. DIESING (1977) Conflict Among Nations: Bargaining, Decision Making, and System Structure in International Crises. Princeton, NJ: Princeton University Press.

SPIEGEL, S. (1979) "The United States and the Arab-Israeli dispute," pp. 336-365 in K. Oye et al. (eds.) Eagle Entangled: U.S. Foreign Policy in a Complex World. New York: Longman.

SULLIVAN, M. (1976) International Relations: Theories and Evidence Englewood Cliffs, NJ: Prentice-Hall.

TAYLOR, A.J.P. (1954) The Struggle for Mastery in Europe 1848-1918. New York: Oxford University Press.

––– (1955/1967) Bismarck: The Man and the Statesman. New York: Vintage.

TANTER, R. (1966) "Dimensions of conflict behavior within and between nations, 1958-1960." Journal of Conflict Resolution 10: 41-64.

THIBAUT, J. and H. H. KELLEY (1959) The Social Psychology of Groups. New York: John Wiley.

WALLACE, M. D. (1971) "Power, status and international war." Journal of Peace Research 8: 23-36.

––– (1973) "Alliance Polarization, cross-cutting and international war 1815-1964: a measurement procedure and some preliminary evidence." Journal of Conflict Resolution 17, 4: 575-604.

––– (1979) "Arms races and escalation." Journal of Conflict Resolution 23: 3-16.

WALLER, B. (1974) Bismarck at the Crossroads: The Reorientation of German Foreign Policy After the Congress of Berlin 1878-1880. New York: Athlone.

WALTZ, K. N. (1979) Theory of International Politics. Reading, Addison-Wesley.

––– (1964) "The stability of a bipolar world,". Daedalus 93: 881-909.

WEHLER, H. (1970) "Bismarck's Imperialism 1862-1890." Past and Present 48: 119-155.

WILKENFELD, J. (1968) "Domestic and foreign conflict behavior of nations." Journal of Peace Research 1: 56-69.

––– (1969) "Some further findings regarding the domestic and foreign conflict behavior of nations." Journal of Peace Research 2: 147-156.

WRIGHT, Q. (1942) A Study of War. Chicago: University of Chicago Press.

ZINNES, D. A. (1968) "The expression and perception of hostility in prewar crisis: 1914," pp. 85-122 in J. D. Singer (ed.) Quantitative International Politics: Insights and Evidence. New York: Free Press.

――― (1972) "Some evidence relevant to the man-milieu hypothesis," pp. 209-251 in
    J. Rosenau et al. (eds.) The Analysis of International Politics. New York: Free
    Press.
ZINNES, D. A., R. ZINNES, and J. L. McCLURE (1972) "Hostility in diplomatic
    communications: a study of the 1914 crisis," pp. 139-162 in C. F. Hermann (ed.)
    International Crisis: Evidence from Behavioral Research. New York: Free Press.

ABOUT THE AUTHOR

Alan S. Alexandroff received his B.A., *cum laude* and with distinction in all subjects, from Cornell University in Government, his M.A. in International History from the London School of Economics and Political Science, and his Ph.D. in Government from Cornell University. While at Cornell completing his graduate studies, he worked as a research associate on the Situational Analysis Project. In 1977, he was appointed to the Department of Political Studies, Queen's University, Kingston Ontario. There, as an Assistant Professor, he teaches courses in American and Soviet foreign policy, international political economy (specifically the politics of money and trade), and international security. Professor Alexandroff is currently preparing a volume with his colleague, Professor James de Wilde of Queen's, on transitional industrial states. Professor Alexandroff is also completing research on the domestic process of going to war, a project funded by the S.S.H.R.C., and he is preparing an article on hegemony or pluralism in the international monetary system, 1961-1976.